NEVER
underestimate
YOUR
teachers

ASCD MEMBER BOOK

Many ASCD members received this book as a
member benefit upon its initial release.

Learn more at: **www.ascd.org/memberbooks**

NEVER

underestimate

YOUR
teachers

INSTRUCTIONAL LEADERSHIP
for EXCELLENCE in
EVERY CLASSROOM

Robyn R. Jackson

Alexandria, Virginia USA

1703 N. Beauregard St. • Alexandria, VA 22311-1714 USA
Phone: 800-933-2723 or 703-578-9600 • Fax: 703-575-5400
Website: www.ascd.org • E-mail: member@ascd.org
Author guidelines: www.ascd.org/write

Gene R. Carter, *Executive Director;* MC Desrosiers, *Chief Program Development Officer;*
Richard Papale, *Publisher;* Genny Ostertag, *Acquisitions Editor;* Julie Houtz, *Director,
Book Editing & Production;* Katie Martin, *Editor;* Louise Bova, *Senior Graphic Designer;*
Mike Kalyan, *Production Manager;* Cindy Stock, *Typesetter;* Kyle Steichen, *Production
Specialist*

All web links in this book are correct as of the publication date below but may have
become inactive or otherwise modified since that time. If you notice a deactivated or
changed link, please e-mail books@ascd.org with the words "Link Update" in the subject
line. In your message, please specify the web link, the book title, and the page number
on which the link appears.

ASCD Member Book, No. FY13-7 (May 2013, P). ASCD Member Books mail to Premium
(P), Select (S), and Institutional Plus (I+) members on this schedule: Jan., PSI+; Feb., P;
Apr., PSI+; May, P; July, PSI+; Aug., P; Sept., PSI+; Nov., PSI+; Dec., P. Select membership
was formerly known as Comprehensive membership.

PAPERBACK ISBN: 978-1-4166-1528-6   ASCD product #110028
Also available as an e-book (see Books in Print for the ISBNs).

Quantity discounts: 10–49 copies, 10%; 50+ copies, 15%; for 1,000 or more copies, call
800-933-2723, ext. 5634, or 703-575-5634. For desk copies: www.ascd.org/deskcopy

Library of Congress Cataloging-in-Publication Data

Jackson, Robyn Renee, author.
    Never underestimate your teachers : instructional leadership for excellence in every
classroom / Robyn R. Jackson.
        pages cm
    Includes bibliographical references and index.
    ISBN 978-1-4166-1528-6 (pbk. : alk. paper) 1. School management and organization.
2. Educational leadership. 3. Teaching. 4. Learning. I. Title.
    LB2805.J15 2013
    371.2—dc23
                                                                        2013002389

22 21 20 19 18 17 16 15 14 13   1 2 3 4 5 6 7 8 9 10 11 12

To Sheri,
who is still very much the boss of me.

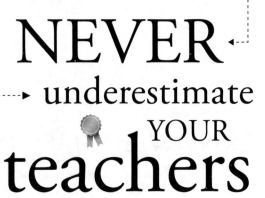

NEVER underestimate YOUR teachers

ACKNOWLEDGMENTS

It is fitting to start a book on leadership by thanking the people who have faithfully provided leadership to me.

I have been blessed to know and be close to my grandparents well into adulthood. I am so grateful to have had the chance to learn from John F. Jackson II, Grace Kilby Jackson, Robert T. Colbert, and Dorothy Colbert. I miss them very much.

I thank God daily for my parents. I happen to have two of the best parents anyone could have. They taught me to be the leader that I am, and I value their loving guidance. I am blessed to have shared my parents with an amazing sister. I don't exaggerate when I say that she truly encompasses all that is good and right and wise in the world. My family keeps me anchored and makes it possible for me to do all that I do. I wouldn't be me without them.

Beyond my family, I've been blessed to be surrounded by some really smart people. I am grateful to the Mindsteps leadership team that has taught me so much about great teaching and instructional leadership. I continue to learn from Sharon Fogler, Dianne Hamilton, Beverly Brandon-Simms, Robin Kinney, John Jackson, Valda Valbrun, Jo-Jo Jackson, and Sheri Jackson. I am also indebted to my personal group of masterminds—Diane MacEachern, Lynn Miller, Betsy Garside, and Perry Pigeon Hooks—who continue to push and inspire me, and to Doug Shiffman, who keeps me focused on what's important. This book would not be what it is without the leadership of Genny Ostertag and Katie Martin, my editors at ASCD. I love working with them.

Finally, I want to thank Charles D. Brooks II, to whose careful and loving leadership I gladly submit. I'd follow him anywhere.

INTRODUCTION: *ANY TEACHER?*

If we truly believe that all children can learn, then we must believe that all educators can learn, even in the face of contrary evidence.

—*Roland S. Barth, On Common Ground*

My conviction that any teacher can become a master teacher tends to provoke certain reactions. Some people smile indulgently and murmur something about the naiveté of youth. "You'll learn," they say. Others are taken aback by the boldness of the statement. "Any teacher?" they ask incredulously, while shaking their heads. "You haven't met some of the teachers in *my* building." Still others eye me suspiciously, as if I am some sort of huckster offering them a sip of snake oil to wash down a handful of magic beans.

Even those who agree with me in principle want to revise the statement. "I'd say *most* teachers," they say cautiously. "Not every teacher is going to become a master teacher."

This is the perspective that defines much of the professional development for educational leaders. It's why we focus more on helping teachers fix aspects of practice than on helping them pursue limitless excellence. It explains why entire curricula and school programs have been built on the idea that student achievement can somehow be teacher-proofed. And this habit of underestimating our teachers is what drives so many administrators and reformers to spend more time talking about getting rid of bad teachers than they do about transforming them into good ones. It seems that while we gladly embrace the idea that all children can learn successfully, we do not extend the same idealism to our colleagues. Any child can learn, but the adults? Well, that's another story.

The tendency is to separate teachers into two categories: the silk purses and the sow's ears. Although we acknowledge that a silk purse may occasionally turn out to be a sow's ear, rarely does it happen the other way around. It's as if we believe that teaching skill is a static gift: everyone is born with a certain amount, and it can't be taught. But this idea creates a bizarre schism. The foundation of our work as educators is that we believe in the human potential to learn, to get better, to grow. Why do we embrace that fundamental belief when it comes to our students and yet reject it as unrealistic when it comes to our colleagues?

Maybe it's because, in the experience of most of us, the really great teachers are a rare breed. Saying that any teacher can become a master teacher seems to sully the idea of masterful teaching, making it, well, *common*. And yet, shouldn't masterful teaching be common? Shouldn't every student have the benefit of a master teacher?

Why Master Teachers?

While we're asking questions, why are master teachers so important, anyway? Does everyone have to be exceptional? Won't a pretty good teacher or even a not-so-bad teacher do?

These are legitimate questions, and in order to answer them we must look at what we mean when we say "master teacher." The quickest definition is that a master teacher is one who helps every student in the classroom meet or exceed the standards. Every student. The master teacher's approach to teaching is seamless. Master teachers seem to instinctively know what to do to help each child learn. They have a large repertoire of skills, and they know when and how to deploy these skills to best help their students.

Master teachers consistently get at least a year's worth of growth out of a year's worth of school; some researchers even argue that master teachers can help students make twice as much progress as an average teacher can (Hanushek, 2004). With an average teacher, a student who begins the year reading at a 3rd grade level might end the year reading at an early 4th grade level. Not bad—and certainly preferable to spending the year with an ineffective teacher and finishing the year still reading at a 3rd grade level. But put that student in a master teacher's class, and by the end of the year, he will be reading at a late 4th grade level and possibly at a 5th grade level. Over time, having a master teacher can make up for disadvantages such as family background and poor early educational experiences. In fact, a student who has a master teacher five years in a row prior to 7th grade can overcome the average mathematics achievement gap that exists between lower- and higher-income students.

So, given the difference masterful teaching makes in students' learning, I'll ask again: Why shouldn't masterful teaching be the goal—the attainable goal—of every teacher in the profession? And why shouldn't promoting masterful teaching be a goal of every school leader? It should be, and it could be. And the very first step is to stop underestimating our teachers. Great instructional leadership means rejecting the idea of masterful teaching as a gift endowed to a select few. It means seeing masterful teaching for what it really is: a combination of skills and attitudes that can be learned . . . and that can be taught.

The Test of Leadership

Leadership is not so much getting people to follow you as it is working through other people to accomplish the vision and goals of the institution. Just as teachers might be judged by how well they handle their most challenging students, we school leaders can be judged by how we handle our most challenging teachers. It is easy to lead those who want to be led, but being able to lead those who initially resist? That's the ultimate test of leadership.

I learned this lesson the hard way (ironically enough, as I was writing this book). Some things to know about me: I was a pretty good middle school administrator. I have coached hundreds of principals, assistant principals, headmasters, deans, and central office administrators on how to help any teacher become a master teacher. I have written a book

(Jackson, 2008) that provides step-by-step guidance on how to have difficult conversations with teachers. And I regularly give speeches on the topic, write articles, and offer advice to administrators who are frustrated and down to their last straw. It would be reasonable to think that I would know exactly what to do if my own leadership were tested, right?

Wrong.

Mrs. Quinton* was a difficult teacher, and she defied my ability to help her. Her problem was not that she didn't know how to teach; it was that she was interested in teaching only certain students—the bright, motivated ones who were already eager to learn. For years, she had been considered one of the best teachers at her school, and she had long occupied a leadership position on the staff. Her colleagues were fiercely loyal to her because she did them little favors; they would not change unless she said so, even if they believed that changing was best for the school. When it came to dealing with Mrs. Quinton, the principal had thrown up his hands. He was afraid to get on her bad side because he knew that if he did, he would lose the cooperation of his entire staff. They would pick her over him.

Enter me. The leadership expert. The fancy paid consultant, brought in to help this school increase rigor in every classroom.

At first, I tried to befriend Mrs. Quinton and convince her that the kind of changes I had in mind would be good for the school. She agreed with me in principle but had very different ideas of how to implement change. In fact, she only wanted to make marginal adjustments to the way things were run, which basically amounted to no change at all. So I tried to work around her, talking with other teachers and providing them resources. Many of them would agree with me in private conversation and make plans to run their classrooms differently, only to change their minds after talking with her.

One morning, after a particularly difficult interaction with Mrs. Quinton, I headed to the principal's office in a huff, my head full of how impossible she was and how she was poisoning the attitudes of the rest of the staff. I was ready to tell him it was time for her to go. But when I sat down in his office, I noticed a copy of my book, *The Instructional Leader's Guide to Strategic Conversations with Teachers*, sitting on his desk. How could I

---

*The teachers and principals you'll meet in this book are all real people, not composites. Unless otherwise noted, their names and a few distinguishing details have been changed.

tell him to get rid of this teacher when my book made the case that every teacher could be "moved and improved"? How could I say that Mrs. Quinton was impossible to work with when I had provided templates that purported to help any leader work with any teacher?

The easy thing to do would have been to get rid of her. But doing that would have seriously damaged the school culture, which would itself have impeded the school's progress. Instead, the principal and I formulated a new plan to work with Mrs. Quinton. When all was said and done, we helped her not only embrace the changes we were trying to make at the school but also improve her own instructional practice and become a much more reflective teacher.

When we become instructional leaders, we don't stop being teachers. The difference is that now we teach *through* other people. Our biggest leadership challenge is not that *we* don't know what to do to increase student success; our biggest challenge is that we must get our teachers to do it.

Your school is only as good as your worst teacher. What's more, *you* are only as good as your ability to handle your worst teacher. Many books on leadership focus on rigorously examining data, developing a vision, and building a proper organizational infrastructure in order to make schools more effective. And they're right. These things are important, and they can be powerful. Yet if you do all that and cannot communicate your vision and your plans to the people who must carry them out, if you cannot inspire teachers to change, if you cannot monitor and give feedback in a way that will ensure that change happens, then you will never get the results you are seeking.

We all have in our heads the image of the school leader who has such a compelling vision, such a strong personality, that the school changes in spite of itself. But the truth is much more boring than that: If you want to move your school forward, you have to move the people in it. If you want excellent instruction in every classroom, you have to help every teacher become an excellent instructor.

Using This Book

In the pages to come, you will learn a process for helping every teacher become a master teacher—a process that I have developed over the past

10 years in my work as an instructional coach, school administrator, and educational consultant. It is the result of the lessons I've learned as I've helped principals, assistant principals, central office leaders, instructional coaches, and superintendents grapple with the very real challenges they face in their urban, suburban, and rural schools throughout the United States. The strategies I'll be sharing have worked time and time again, and if you really want to move your teachers and your school forward, this is the work you must do.

Never Underestimate Your Teachers does not address developing a mission statement or communicating your vision to your staff. It won't teach you how to set goals and achieve them. There are other books that do a good job of showing you how to do those things—all of which are important in leading a school. But this book is not about leading a school; it's about leading teachers.

Over the course of six chapters, I am going to show you how to recognize good teaching and what to do if you aren't seeing it in the classroom. We'll look at evaluation as something undertaken not to identify and get rid of bad teachers but to help bad ones become good, good ones become great, and great ones become even greater. You will learn how to meet these teachers where they are and, through a series of supports, help them all move forward. I'll share real-life stories of how I and other school leaders have tackled the kinds of challenges you face in your school. Many of the skills and strategies we used are ones you already know; what you'll learn is how to leverage those skills and strategies to make a real impact.

Chapter 1 provides the foundation for this knowledge, deconstructing what good teaching really is and how it incorporates both *teacher skill* and *teacher will.* The chapters that follow examine how you can affect both of these aspects so that over time your teachers get better and better at what they do. You'll find "Yes, but . . ." sections designed to address common concerns and "Takeaways" that summarize each chapter's key points—and are perfect for sharing with other members of your instructional leadership team. Finally, Chapter 6 discusses how to bring all the strategies you have learned together to shape a professional culture at your school where every teacher is on a sure pathway to masterful teaching and, as a result, every student is on a surer pathway to success.

If you are an instructional coach, you'll learn strategies for helping teachers grow and want to grow. You'll learn how to help teachers prepare for and respond to observations and evaluations and how to inspire and support all the teachers you serve to work toward mastery. If you are a teacher leader (i.e., a department head, a team leader, a lead teacher), you'll learn strategies for moving your team forward toward team and school goals. You'll also learn how to straddle the dual roles of teacher and leader in a way that best supports the teachers you serve. If you are a school-based administrator, you'll learn how to move your entire school toward a professional culture that is focused on masterful teaching, and how to help each of your teachers ultimately get there. You'll learn specific strategies for facilitating the observation process and helping teachers use the observation process to grow toward mastery. And, if you are a district leader, you'll learn how to best support the schools you lead so that every teacher in every school is continuously improving. You'll also learn strategies that will help you design and implement a teacher evaluation process that truly improves teaching and learning. No matter which of these roles is yours, you'll learn how to identify what is important for teachers to focus on and how to develop better teachers and, ultimately, better schools.

To help you succeed in this very important work, this book's Appendix contains several other tools to help you put what you are learning into practice, including diagnostics you can use to help you determine a teacher's skill level and prime motivator and to determine your own prime motivator as well. We have also created a companion website at www.mindstepsinc.com/lead so that we can share even more tools, tips, and strategies.

After reading this book, you'll know exactly how to assess and move the teachers you serve toward mastery. You'll have a plan for getting started and all the tools you need to make it work. And you'll know how to access other resources to support and sustain your work over time. In short, you'll have everything you need to build and lead master teachers.

Now, let's get to work.

1

WHAT IS MASTERFUL
TEACHING?

Experiences where you are forced to slow down, make errors, and correct them—as you would if you were walking up an ice-covered hill, slipping and stumbling as you go—end up making you swift and graceful without your realizing it.

—Daniel Coyle, *The Talent Code*

Walk into Mr. Ishigowa's* classroom and you wouldn't be impressed. There are no objectives written on the board. The bulletin boards display no student work. In fact, the walls are bare, save an ancient poster of Einstein and a chart illustrating different geometric shapes. Watching Mr. Ishigowa teach, you wonder why his students—mostly minority boys, with pants hanging well below their waists and baseball caps pulled low over their eyes—are even paying attention. Mr. Ishigowa doesn't wow his students with dramatic lectures or entertain them with beguiling stories. He doesn't group them into jigsaws or dream up clever games for them to play. He just teaches math. For 45 straight minutes he is at the board writing formulas, explaining angles, showing students how to calculate the

---

*The master teachers in this chapter are called by their real names.

slope of a line. Short, bespectacled, and thin; bald, save for a few wisps of gray hair that stick up on top; and wearing pants pulled up almost to his chest, Mr. Ishigowa's physical presence defies the image of a master teacher. So does his quiet manner and heavily accented speech. And yet . . . he can take any student—even students who have failed geometry twice, even fourth-year freshmen—and help them pass the state geometry test. Mr. Ishigowa is a master teacher.

In Mrs. Meneker's classroom, music blares from the stereo on her desk. Half of the student desks are pushed casually against the far wall. Few if any of her 11th graders are sitting down, though: They are standing in corners talking or hunched over tables coloring while occasionally sipping sodas. Some are slouched in a row of beanbag chairs along the back wall of the classroom, eating chips and laughing as they flip through magazines. Mrs. Meneker works with one student at her desk, while the other 29 seem to be on their own.

But look more closely: The students standing in the corner aren't just talking; they're looking at a map and debating the value of the Louisiana Purchase. Those students coloring? They're drawing maps of what the United States looked like before and after the Louisiana Purchase, discussing different possibilities for dividing the states, and debating which should be slave states and which should be free states—and using their maps to bolster their point. The students slouched in the beanbag chairs reading? They are looking through collections of political cartoons from the time and selecting which they will address in an argumentative essay. Mrs. Meneker and the student at her desk are reviewing the student's last test results and setting long-term goals for the next assessment. Before the week is over, Mrs. Meneker will have a similar meeting with all of her other students. Even though some struggle now because they aren't really prepared for the class, by the end of the year, all of them will pass the AP exam with at least a score of 3. Mrs. Meneker is a master teacher.

Mrs. Marshall doesn't work with students after school. She doesn't stay in class during lunch and work with them, either. She doesn't give make-up work and rarely offers extra credit. Her gradebook has few grades in it. When she lectures to her 6th and 7th graders, she does so from the front of the classroom using nothing but a short list of topics written on the chalkboard—no PowerPoint, no interactive whiteboard, no video, no technology at all. At the beginning of her lecture, she tells her students, "I am not a tape recorder, and there is no rewind button on me, so you will have to pay attention." After the lecture, her students work on their assignment sheets—and there is an assignment sheet almost every day. When asked, she will tell you that her students determine their own grades. If they want to pass, they will pass; if they want to fail, that is their choice as well. Every one of Mrs. Marshall's students signs a learning contract for each unit of study. They are required to do a certain number of assignments, and if they do them, they earn a *C* for the unit. Those who want to earn a higher grade complete extra assignments according to the contract. And although the "choice to fail" is up to the student, few if any of them ever make that choice. Mrs. Marshall is a master teacher.

In Mr. Davis's classroom the students, all male, sit in rows—razor-straight rows, facing the board. They raise their hands for permission to sharpen their pencils; often, their requests are denied. Mr. Davis doesn't like a lot of movement in his classroom. He refers to his 4th graders by their last names and insists that they refer to him as "Sir." Mr. Davis runs a tight ship. At first, it seems a bit much for 9- and 10-year-olds. After all, they are still children, and such military precision seems a little draconian. But for this group of boys, the structure helps them focus on planning the class garden using sophisticated tables based on average rainfall, crop yield, and the merits of organic compost over commercial fertilizer. The structure helps them concentrate on developing their own hypotheses about the optimal time to plant and whether it is better to start the seeds in a pot in the classroom or plant them directly in the soil. The structure helps them resist using yardsticks as swords rather than using them to measure the proper size of their lot. And the structure helps them develop the self-discipline to work independently or in small groups without becoming distracted. They're learning to think like scientists. Mr. Davis is a master teacher.

If I were to ask you to close your eyes right now and picture a master teacher, odds are that you wouldn't conjure up Mr. Ishigowa, Mrs. Meneker, Mrs. Marshall, or Mr. Davis. We each have a sense of what a master teacher "looks like" and what a master teacher does. And yet in classrooms all around the world there are teachers doing a masterful job of helping students meet or exceed the standards who don't look at all like what we would imagine and who may not engage in the laundry list of best practices we would expect. There are also many teachers out there who conform exactly to our personal "master teacher" schema and yet have students who are making little to no progress and may even be consistently failing.

We need a better schema.

What Is Teaching?

Before we pin down what masterful teaching is, we should backtrack to consider teaching in general. All teaching is a combination of skill and will.

Skill is the science of teaching; it involves a teacher's pedagogical and content knowledge. It determines how well teachers know the subject and how well they can help students learn it. *Will* has to do with a teacher's passion; it is the art of teaching. It involves teachers' drive to help all students be successful. Master teachers have high skill and high will. They don't just know their craft; they also have the drive and determination to be the best at it.

Because teaching is such a complex act, cursory feedback and standardized support can never help teachers grow to the master level. Unless you understand both their skill and their will, you cannot provide the targeted help that they need. Rather than rely on Hollywood images of effective teaching or our own notions of what good teaching should look like (based on how we were taught or what we ourselves did as teachers), assessing a teacher's effectiveness requires a much more objective and comprehensive idea of what masterful teaching looks like and how it incorporates both skill and will.

Teacher Skill

As noted, the skill component of masterful teaching comprises both content knowledge and pedagogy. Teachers who understand content but cannot figure out how to help students understand it cannot be effective in the classroom. Neither can teachers who know several strategies for helping students learn but not how to apply these strategies in different situations and tailor them to all learners, or teachers who are excellent instructional designers but poor classroom managers. Pedagogy and content-area knowledge are intricately intertwined and cannot be separated into two distinct categories; teachers must have *both* to be considered skillful.

Teacher skill is rooted in the seven principles of effective instruction (Jackson, 2009), a concept we will explore in greater detail in Chapter 2. In short, though, highly skilled teachers start where their students are, know where students are going, expect to get them there, support them along the way, use feedback to help themselves and their students get better, focus on quality not quantity, and never work harder than their students. As a result, highly skilled teachers are good planners. They know how to structure a lesson and a unit to ensure that students learn and understand the material. They plan both formative and summative assessments and use the feedback these assessments render to adjust their instruction throughout the unit. Those with high levels of skill structure lessons so that learning becomes inevitable rather than accidental. They understand how to sequence instruction, how to anticipate student confusion, and how to explain difficult concepts in ways that help students develop increasing understanding over time. They know different ways to explain concepts and how to match their collection of instructional strategies to individual students' needs.

Another essential component of teacher skill is classroom management: knowing how to structure the classroom so that students can focus on learning. When inappropriate behaviors distract students, highly skilled teachers know how to help students quickly get back on track. They know how to balance structure and support with autonomy and how to help students take responsibility for and ownership of their own learning and behavior over time.

Teacher Will

The *will* component of masterful teaching is rooted in the desire to help all students learn and the determination to ensure that all students *do* learn. It's more than simple motivation, however; will encompasses a teacher's entire attitude and approach to teaching and to students. It's what powers a teacher to find ways to reach students even in the face of huge obstacles. It's about persistence, trying strategy after strategy until one succeeds. Teachers with very high levels of will see teaching not as a job but as a vocation.

Will is what drives the teachers who continually refine and hone their craft, reflect on practice, and embrace data and feedback. It's why these teachers set high expectations of themselves and their students, why they are not content with the status quo. They want their students to keep growing and reaching, and they model that in their own practice. Teachers with high levels of teaching will understand the importance of relationships and work hard to make sure that every student in the room is safe, engaged, and connected.

An individual teacher's will is affected by countless factors, including working conditions, personal problems, relationships with colleagues, passion about a particular subject, district constraints, school climate, and student attitudes. Will can fluctuate throughout the course of a career, a school year, or even a day. Teachers often start their careers with high will but, because they don't receive the right kind of support, become discouraged and frustrated and lose their will over time. Conversely, a teacher may begin a school year with low will and meet a group of students that is so inspirational that the teacher's will skyrockets during the course of the year. Teaching will is not static and must constantly be nurtured if it is to be sustained.

The Will/Skill Matrix: Where the Path to Professional Development Begins

Given that teaching comprises both skill and will, and that teachers possess varying degrees of each, considering where an individual teacher falls on a simple matrix of skill level and will level (see Figure 1.1) gives us a new way to think about that teacher's professional development needs.

The matrix allows us to identify four teacher profiles or "types"—*high will/low skill, low will/low skill, high will/high skill,* and *low will/high skill*—and these designations offer an approach to the analysis and development

Figure 1.1   The Will/Skill Matrix

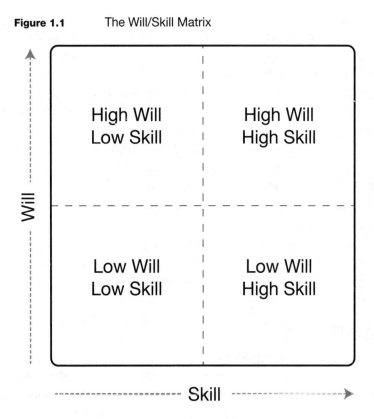

of masterful teaching that is far more useful than the familiar stereotypes and the same old received wisdom. Each type of teacher has a different set of needs and, thus, needs a different type of instructional leadership. Understanding where teachers in your school fall on the Will/Skill Matrix will help you identify a leadership approach that directly addresses their individual needs.

Let's take an initial look at the four general types. You'll learn more about each in the pages to come.

High Will/Low Skill

High-will/low-skill teachers are often enthusiastic about teaching. They know that they have areas they need to work on, and they want to improve. They often seek out a supervisor's feedback, enthusiastically participate in professional development, and try new strategies or ideas in their classrooms. But because their practice is not rooted in principles, their reliance on strategies makes their instruction disjointed.

High-will/low-skill teachers tend to be new to the profession. However, veteran teachers who have not found ways to integrate their teaching knowledge over time can also fit the profile. High-will/low-skill teachers often have very lofty ideals about teaching, which unfortunately can lead them to implementing instructional strategies that do students more harm than good. Or, in their eagerness to improve, they may try out several instructional strategies without giving much thought as to appropriateness for their students.

High-will/low-skill teachers are willing to learn. With the right kind of support, they can quickly get better. The danger is that without the right kind of support, these teachers can quickly lose their enthusiasm and become low-will/low-skill teachers.

Low Will/Low Skill

Low-will/low-skill teachers have, in many ways, simply given up. They see teaching as a job rather than as a profession or a calling. Many are "retired on the job" or are biding their time until they can move on to other things. They "phone it in" and do not seem invested in their craft.

Low-will/low-skill teachers do not buck the status quo; theirs is a more passive resistance to change. They tend to stay out of the way and do only what is absolutely necessary and no more. They do not volunteer for additional duties. They participate marginally on teams, letting others take on the bulk of the work, and passively attend meetings without contributing anything. They work hard at being invisible.

In some ways, the low-will/low-skill teacher is the most difficult to move toward mastery. It's very challenging to try to address both will and skill at the same time, so you need to determine which to take on first. If it appears that low will has resulted in low skill, it makes sense to work on will first. But other times these teachers have lost their will over time because they have been repeatedly unsuccessful in the classroom. In that case, it makes sense to work on their skill first; as they become more successful in the classroom, their will increases.

High Will/High Skill

High-will/high-skill teachers are master teachers. They are adept at both the art and the science of teaching. Not only are they highly motivated and committed to their students' success, but they have the knowledge and skill to make their students successful.

High-will/high-skill teachers operate according to the principles of effective instruction. They have integrated their practice to the point where it seems that they instinctively know the right thing to do. But they are not content to rest on their laurels. Their high will means that they are constantly refining their practice, learning new ways to reach students, and seeking input and feedback from others to hone their craft.

The danger with high-will/high-skill teachers is that without the right kind of leadership and support, they can become bored and seek new opportunities elsewhere, or become frustrated and grow cynical over time. Because they are so effective with students, they take on more responsibilities or work with the most challenging students. Many want to do a good job and will work hard even in the most impossible of circumstances, but over time they can become burned out. In that case, a valuable high-will/high-skill teacher can become a low-will/high-skill teacher.

Low Will/High Skill

Low-will/high-skill teachers understand the science of teaching but have neglected the art. They know their subjects and have fairly decent pedagogy, but they lack the soft skills that make teaching truly masterful. They have the skills to be effective teachers, but for a variety of reasons they simply do not do what is best for their students.

Because they are fairly effective teachers, they may have an inflated view of their own practice. They may think that because they have to some degree mastered many of the skills of teaching they have mastered teaching itself. This makes them particularly unreceptive to feedback, especially if it highlights areas where their practice needs improving.

Low-will/high-skill teachers can sometimes become the saboteurs of the school and of any attempt at change. Because they don't feel that they need any improvement, they may actively resist efforts to provide feedback, institute reforms, or start new programs—often to the detriment of students. They also can become very cynical, identifying ways that this strategy or that reform won't work rather than finding ways to make it work.

The good news is that many low-will/high-skill teachers started out as high-will/high-skill teachers who experienced some disappointment or frustration that has sapped them of their will. Thus, there is every reason to believe that with the right kind of leadership and support they will once again function at the master teacher level.

It is important to understand that a teacher's "type" is fluid. Teachers may shift from one quadrant to the next as they move through their careers, change courses or subjects, switch schools, move to different grade levels, work on different teams, or experience different events in their personal lives. Thus, you cannot label a teacher as one teacher type and expect that label to still apply in a few months or years. To truly help every teacher become a master teacher, you have to be aware of what quadrant they occupy on any particular day, semester, or year. This means continually examining data, both formal and informal, and knowing what to look for.

☑ Checkpoint Summary

Take the first steps toward supporting every teacher's progress toward mastery by figuring out their "type"—where they fall, right now, on the Will/Skill Matrix.

TEACHER TYPE	CHARACTERISTICS	LOOKS LIKE
High will/low skill	Enthusiastic; idealistic; willing to learn	Seeks feedback and explores new strategies and ideas, but implementation is inconsistent and ineffective
Low will/low skill	Discouraged; not invested; "retired on the job"	Does not volunteer or contribute; passive; tries to stay beneath the radar
High will/high skill	Motivated and skillful	Easily identifies and implements appropriate strategies; explores new ideas, seeks feedback, and refines practice; takes on challenges
Low will/high skill	Skillful but disinterested; "seen it all"	Unreceptive to feedback; resists efforts to try new approaches; saboteurs

Leading All Types to Mastery

It is as critical to provide teachers with differentiated leadership as it is to provide students with differentiated instruction. Tailoring your leadership approach to the skill and will of the individuals you are leading is key to helping all teachers embrace change and significantly improve their practice. *Not* tailoring your leadership approach can lead to undue frustration—for you and the teacher—and undermine your leadership goals.

For instance, many leaders make the mistake of trying to solve a will problem with a skill solution. They hope that by providing more and better professional development or providing additional resources, they can raise a teacher's will. Or they take the opposite approach and try to solve a skill problem with a will solution, wasting time trying to inspire a struggling teacher to do better when what that teacher needs is specific help with developing skill. Understanding a teacher's will and skill is not only more efficient, in that you don't waste time on the wrong leadership approach, but also more successful. It helps you identify a targeted approach that will make the biggest difference for your teachers.

In the next few chapters, you will learn strategies for understanding and building teacher skill and will. In the last chapter, you will learn how to put those strategies together to create a strategic leadership approach for the teachers you serve.

YES, BUT . . .
What if a teacher thinks that he is high skill or high will but I think just the opposite?

Sometimes you will assess a teacher's skill or will and come to a conclusion that differs from the teacher's own perception of his skill or will. What do you do when you run across a teacher whose self-assessment seems inaccurate or downright delusional?

For starters, remember that you don't ever have to share your assessment of a teacher's will or skill with the teacher. It's a tool for you, intended to guide your approach, your work.

You also don't have to convince a teacher of his low skill or will in order to help him; the strategies you'll read about in the chapters to come are designed to work even for teachers who think they are closer to mastery than they really are. So don't get caught up in convincing teachers to assess their own will and skill in the same way that you have, and take heart that the kind of support you provide will help them develop a more accurate self-assessment over time.

CHAPTER 1 TAKEAWAYS
Understanding Teacher Skill and Teacher Will

CONSIDER	KEY QUESTION	INDICATORS OF HIGH SKILL	INDICATORS OF HIGH WILL
Observational data	*What does the teacher's instructional practice look like?*	• Posts objectives and essential questions. • Uses classroom management strategies that are effective and consistent. • Uses instructional strategies effectively.	• Interacts well with students (responding to questions, supporting a range of learners, using motivational strategies, and encouraging student engagement).
Feedback	*How does the teacher respond to feedback?*	• Implements suggestions or otherwise acts on feedback.	• Engages in reflective conversations about feedback.
Teacher artifacts	*What instructional materials has the teacher produced, and how do they align with the standards, the curriculum, and the learning needs of the students?*	• Designs lesson plans, assessments, and assignments that align with standards, are appropriate for students' ability levels, and reflect sound pedagogy.	• Communicates with parents and comments on student papers and products. • Sets and follows classroom rules, policies, and procedures that support student progress.
Classroom formative assessment tools and data	*How does the teacher create/ use formative assessment?*	• Uses student data/ results to improve instruction and practice. • Aligns assessments with instructional goals and unit objectives.	• Adjusts instruction based on assessment data. • Follows up with individual students regarding their performance and supports students accordingly.

Understanding Teacher Skill and Teacher Will *continued*

CONSIDER	KEY QUESTION	INDICATORS OF HIGH SKILL	INDICATORS OF HIGH WILL
Classroom summative assessment data	*How many of the teacher's students have mastered the standards?*	• Analyzes data/results and targets areas for improvement (students and instructional practice).	• Takes ownership of data/results and uses them to improve instruction.
Informal conversations	*How does the teacher view his or her practice?*	• Understands where students are and what they need to do to move forward. • Has a good sense of pedagogy; instruction is driven by overarching, instructionally sound principles.	• Takes ownership of student progress. • Shows enthusiasm for new ideas. • Likes/enjoys students and families.
Participation on teams, committees	*How does the teacher interact with colleagues?*	• Makes valuable contributions; shares resources. • Implements team feedback in classroom.	• Seeks input from colleagues and is appreciative of support and feedback. • Shares ideas and the work of the team.

2
UNDERSTANDING AND DIAGNOSING SKILL

Every artist was first an amateur.

—*Ralph Waldo Emerson*

Ms. Lane was my first solo teacher observation. I studied the observation instrument ahead of time and memorized its six domains. I reviewed the individual skill ratings for each domain to ensure I understood the differences. I practiced scripting lessons to make sure that I would be able to capture every nuance of what I would be observing in the classroom. I was ready.

During the observation, I recorded every word Ms. Lane said, and I wrote down most of what her students said, too. I copied the objective written on the board, took note of what was displayed on the bulletin boards, drew a diagram of the classroom configuration, and took time to walk around and look over students' shoulders to note what they were working on. I even collected a few teacher artifacts (handouts and assignments) before I left.

Back in my office, I highlighted my notes, first assigning a color to each of the observation instrument's domains and standards and then color-coding the teacher behaviors I had documented. I identified patterns and carefully composed my post-observation write-up. Then I met with Ms. Lane to go over my assessment of her practice. I shared my "data," explained what I thought were trends, sandwiched my suggestions between praise, and backed up everything with examples from the classroom. She nodded along, accepted my write-up, and thanked me pleasantly on her way out.

Alone in my office, I felt a strange sense of disquiet. I knew I had done an excellent job of cataloging teaching behaviors, noting performance patterns, and providing suggestions for follow-up. And yet . . . I wasn't sure I had really *helped*. I later heard that Ms. Lane had complained I was unqualified to speak to her skill or make suggestions for her practice having spent just 30 total minutes in her classroom. The worst part about it was that I suspected she was right.

Diagnosing a teacher's skill level is often presented as a simple thing—just check off a set of right or wrong behaviors on a checklist. But anyone who has spent a lot of time in classrooms knows the limitations of this approach to evaluation. At best, the process of cataloging teaching behaviors and then assigning designations such as *unsatisfactory, proficient,* and *exemplary* allows us to assess a teacher's performance at a very cursory level. Although teaching behaviors can tell us whether or not a teacher meets a benchmark, how close a teacher is to being put on an improvement plan, or even whether or not a teacher will earn tenure, these behaviors alone reveal surprisingly little about a teacher's real skill. That's because teaching behaviors are only the tip of the iceberg—the visible portion of a very complex process.

To teach is to engage in a sophisticated and interlocking set of decisions, all of which have a profound effect on students. A teacher must consider numerous variables and decide, for example, how to present a particular concept, how to structure a conversation, how to incorporate technology, how to work with colleagues, which aspects of content to emphasize, the means of engaging and motivating one student or many students, and so on and so on. In order get a full picture of any teacher's skill, we need an evaluation approach that considers the thinking and underlying principles that drive that teacher's decisions and subsequent classroom behaviors. In short, we need evaluation that focuses on the teacher's mindset.

The Mindset of Skillful Teaching

The mindset that factors so significantly in teaching skill can be best described by looking at the principles for effective teaching. I outline these principles in my book *Never Work Harder Than Your Students and Other Principles of Great Teaching* (Jackson, 2009). There, I also explain why principles trump strategies if one hopes to become a master teacher. Strategies are *what* a teacher does, the actions a teacher takes, the behaviors that can be observed. Principles determine *how* a teacher teaches and how a teacher thinks about teaching; they inform a teacher's actions and behaviors. It's a subtle distinction but an important one for teachers and for school leaders. When you are evaluating a teacher, you want to know if that teacher can reliably deliver results in any situation, not just perform under optimal conditions. You want to know that the decisions that teacher makes will lead to student learning.

The seven principles of effective instruction are as follows:

1. Start where your students are.
2. Know where they are going.
3. Expect to get them there.
4. Support them along the way.
5. Use feedback to help you both get better.
6. Focus on quality, not quantity.
7. Never work harder than your students.

These principles are embedded in most teacher evaluation instruments, but focusing on them specifically and deliberately is a way to cut straight to the thinking that drives teaching decisions so that you can figure out how to help teachers make *better* decisions. For that reason, I have used the principles to categorize teaching practice into four skill levels: *novice, apprentice, practitioner,* and *master teacher.* The levels are not determined by the number of years a teacher has been teaching or even by a score on an evaluation instrument. Instead, each level is characterized by a general mindset and approach to teaching based on how the teacher manifests the seven principles. Together, they function as a continuum: most teachers begin at the novice level and grow over time to the apprentice, the practitioner, and, with the right guidance and support, the master teacher level. It is a journey that is never finished, as teachers continually grow in their practice over the course of their careers.

Differentiating Between Low Skill and High Skill

Because teaching skill functions on a continuum, leaders sometimes find it difficult to categorize teachers as either "low skill" or "high skill." These are broad labels, to be sure, but they are an important starting point. Figure 2.1 compares the characteristics of low-skill and high-skill teachers.

Teachers in the novice or apprentice categories are considered "low skill" in that they still struggle with some of the major aspects of teaching, leading their instruction to be inconsistent, disjointed, and in most cases, less effective than it could be. Practitioners and master teachers, on the other hand, can generally be considered "high skill." Although they may still have challenges, their teaching is largely coherent and effective in helping students meet or exceed standards.

One of the challenges in determining whether a teacher is at the novice, apprentice, practitioner, or master level is that individuals may be proficient or even excel in one aspect of practice and yet struggle in another. No, you really cannot diagnose teaching skill by simply checking off a set of teaching behaviors observed during a 30-minute visit. As noted, observations yield a lot of data, but they do not tell the entire story. To round out your assessment of teacher skill, be sure to make use of the various data collection strategies captured in Chapter 1's Takeaways (see pp. 21–22). Only after you've examined several sources of data—including various student assessments, teacher artifacts, and response to feedback—should you proceed with a skill-level diagnosis.

 Tools to Use

Need more guidance in determining an individual teacher's skill level? See **Tool 1** in the Appendix.

Finally, it's essential to keep in mind that placing a teacher in a skill-level category is a starting point, not an end in itself. Making this diagnosis allows you to design specific, targeted, differentiated professional development. It's a key part of supporting every member of a teaching staff—at every level of skill—and helping them all improve.

Figure 2.1   Common Skill Indicators: Low and High

Low-Skill Teachers . . .	High-Skill Teachers . . .
Struggle with content-area knowledge, cannot anticipate confusion, and make critical subject-area mistakes in content delivery.	Understand the content and can anticipate and clear up areas of confusion.
Ineffectively apply classroom management strategies; students are distracted, disengaged, off task, and unproductive.	Effectively use classroom management strategies to keep students engaged, on task, safe, and productive.
Struggle to keep pace with the curriculum and may leave several units incomplete.	Keep pace with the curriculum by making judicious choices regarding how to balance available time, content, and students' needs.
Show consistently low student test scores with little sign of improvement from students.	Show consistent gains in student test scores over the course of the school year.
Do not respond to data or adjust instruction accordingly.	Collect data and use it to adjust instruction to better meet students' needs.
Implement a grading system that is confusing, inconsistent, or unreasonable.	Thoughtfully develop and implement a grading system that provides students and parents with accurate feedback on students' progress and achievement.
Have little or no strategy for effectively intervening with struggling students.	Proactively intervene with students to help them quickly get back on track.
Fail to understand students and their learning needs and deliver instruction in the same way for every child.	Seek to understand students and their learning needs, and customize instruction to meet students' needs.
Focus on moving through activities and provide instruction that is unrelated to learning goals.	Set rigorous learning objectives and match instruction to best help students meet these objectives.
Plan ineffectively or not at all.	Plan effectively to move students systematically toward learning goals.
Have low expectations and convey these low expectations through below-grade-level assignments and negative interactions with students.	Maintain high expectations for students and effectively communicate these expectations to students.
Focus on covering the curriculum rather than selecting quality learning experiences for students.	Carefully select learning experiences that are best matched to students' interests, needs, and curricular goals.
Ineffectively assess student performance by using assessments that are unrelated.	Develop effective formative and summative assessments and use assessments to help students improve performance.
Have only one strategy for instructional delivery.	Have multiple ways of explaining information and adjust teaching style according to students' needs.
Attempt to control student learning and behavior.	Help students take ownership of their learning and behavior.

Examining the Four Categories of Teaching Skill

With the complexity of skill diagnosis fresh in our minds, let's take a closer look at the four skill-level categories, beginning at the top.

Master Teacher

For master teachers, teaching is fluid and automatic. They just seem to know the right thing to do at the right time. Teaching—good teaching—is almost as natural to them as breathing. Their skill looks like a talent, a gift, something innate.

But what seems effortless and seamless is actually the result of a lot of hard work. Master teachers invest most of their time "up front" on planning and thinking through their teaching goals, unpacking standards and setting learning goals for students that are within but at the outer edge of students' current abilities. Master teachers convey high expectations for students and help students reach toward rigorous learning targets.

Master teachers not only make conscious decisions about what students need to know and how well they need to know it; they also decide early on what evidence of student mastery they will collect. They use both formative and summative assessment to monitor student learning, give students growth-oriented feedback, and adjust their instructional practice to help all students meet or exceed learning goals. When assessments reveal that students aren't learning as they should, master teachers act right away by incorporating supports into their instructional practice to catch students *before* they fail. What's more, this intervention is proactive and systematic, providing students with appropriate supports and then removing those scaffolds as students' proficiency increases over time.

Because master teachers understand both the subject (or subjects) they teach and the relationships among and between key content-area concepts, they can anticipate student confusion. They have a wide range of pedagogical approaches they can match to the varied needs of their students. Master teachers know that not all students learn the same way, and they are able to individualize their instructional approach accordingly. They teach students how to use feedback not only to monitor their own learning but also, ultimately, to identify the ways to learn that are best for them.

Master teachers know how to divide responsibility for learning between themselves and their students. Their lessons are engaging, challenging, relevant, and appropriate for their students' abilities, interests, and curricular goals. Their lesson sequence not only is coherent but also clearly moves students in a steady progression toward unit learning goals and curricular standards and invites students to be co-creators of their learning experiences. Master teachers empower students to take ownership of their own learning. They help students internalize rigorous learning standards, high expectations, and respect for themselves and others and set up learning experiences that allow students to take the lead in their own learning.

Master teachers understand that every student is unique, and they recognize the different interests, values, priorities, talents, and skill sets that each student brings to the classroom. What's more, they are able to help students leverage these personal "currencies" to reach rigorous learning goals. At the same time, master teachers base their expectations not on what they know students can do, but on what they know *they* can do to help their students. Thus, in addition to recognizing and celebrating students' abilities, they also work to help students acquire the additional skills and knowledge needed to successfully navigate the school curriculum and culture.

Master teachers manage their classrooms skillfully and smoothly. They are attuned to the various needs of their students and find efficient ways to individualize their responses to meet these needs. Discipline is unobtrusive and preventative; master teachers generally stop classroom disruptions before they even begin. In the master teacher's classroom, transitions between tasks are seamless; routines and procedures are clear; and discipline is respectful, firm, and individualized, resulting in an environment that is respectful, efficient, and empowering for students.

Although they are highly skilled, usually scoring "highly effective" on most teacher evaluations, master teachers are always looking to learn more. They are reflective about their practice and seek ways to improve. They welcome feedback from students, parents, peers, and supervisors and use this feedback to refine their practice. They also engage in professional learning and action research to inform and improve their instruction. Master teachers are constantly growing.

Practitioner

Teachers at the practitioner level are considered to be good teachers. They have a solid knowledge of the curriculum, a working knowledge of a wide range of pedagogical approaches, and effective classroom management techniques that make their classrooms run smoothly most of the time.

Most veteran teachers score in the practitioner range. They have been teaching for a few years and make conscious choices about what they do in the classroom based on their experience. Although they are proficient in their practice, their approach to teaching isn't entirely seamless, and there are still areas where they need improvement.

Practitioner teachers can unpack curriculum standards and have a solid understanding of their learning goals. Most of their lesson and unit objectives are clear, are rigorous, and convey high expectations, although they occasionally simply teach to the standard. During class, they ask relevant and appropriate questions that foster student thinking, provide clear explanations, and draw students' attention to connections between lesson content, related content, and students' own prior knowledge and experiences. Practitioners don't always anticipate student confusion, but they respond well to students' questions and quickly clear up confusion when they encounter it.

Practitioners choose learning materials and craft assignments with care, and they ensure both are aligned with the instructional goals of the unit. They select instructional approaches that keep students cognitively engaged and work hard to differentiate instruction to accommodate the various learning needs of their students.

Practitioners align their assessments to their learning goals most of the time and work to make assessment criteria clear and accessible to students. They use the feedback they get from formative and summative assessment to adjust their instructional approach and provide interventions. However, they do not always provide students with the growth-oriented feedback that will allow students to take charge and improve their performance on their own.

Teachers at the practitioner level intervene with struggling students but may not always do so before students begin to fail. This means that although most students in practitioners' classes get the support they need, some face a difficult path, because the initial intervention comes after they have already gone off track.

Practitioners are realistic about their students. They are aware of students' strengths, challenges, and learning needs, and they believe that they can make a difference for their students regardless of economic, social, and learning challenges. But practitioners tend to place more faith in the positive alignment of outside factors (good curriculum plus solid instructional strategies plus smart planning protocols) than they do in their own ability to teach well in any circumstance. They know and use a host of resources, and tend to focus on choosing the right solution rather than creating an individualized solution for their students.

Practitioners recognize and appreciate the currencies students bring with them to the classroom, although they do tend to focus more on helping students acquire new currencies (e.g., what they value personally and believe to be the "right ways" to do school) than on showing students how to use the currencies they already have to achieve excellent results. Practitioners also tend to adjust their instructional approach to accommodate groups of students (e.g., students who are learning English, advanced students, or struggling learners) rather than individualizing their approach based on each student's needs.

Practitioners like and respect their students. Their classroom interactions demonstrate real care and concern. They communicate genuine enthusiasm for the subject matter they teach, and they set high standards for students. But even though practitioners convey high expectations for student learning, their students don't necessarily internalize these high expectations. Students tend to depend on the teacher to set standards and goals rather than take complete ownership of their own learning. Although practitioners will often set rigorous standards that push students to aim beyond their current abilities, they will also step in to "rescue" students when they perceive the work is becoming "too challenging."

Classroom management for practitioners is efficient and effective, with very little loss of instructional time. Transitions between activities are smooth, clear routines are in place and adhered to most of the time, and behavioral expectations are clear and generally met. Disruptions are minimal, and when practitioners do have to discipline students, they enforce clear consequences and are able to quickly redirect student behavior and get students back on task. In general, students are engaged and productive most of the time.

Practitioners have a broad repertoire of instructional strategies, but these strategies may not always be fully assimilated into their practice. Thus, although their teaching is generally smooth, it is not entirely seamless. Still, practitioners are very skilled in both content and pedagogy, work hard to master their craft, and are generally effective with most students. They tend to score "effective" on most evaluation instruments.

Apprentice

For an apprentice teacher, good teaching is a matter of having the right strategy. They take time to understand curriculum objectives and figure out how to meet them all, but they tend to attack each objective separately and miss interrelationships and how each objective contributes to the big picture of student learning. As a result, the lessons of apprentice teachers often lack coherence.

Apprentice teachers have a limited range of instructional approaches, and not all of them are appropriate for the discipline, grade level, or students they teach. They are usually aware of the value of differentiation but base their choice of instructional strategies on group considerations— what seems likely to work with "high," "on-level," and "low" students— rather than on individual student needs.

Apprentices use generally appropriate assessments but in a perfunctory manner. Their goals for assessment are not entirely clear, their assessment format may not echo their instructional approach, or the assessment itself may not address all the content covered. They do not consistently use assessment results to provide feedback for students or to inform their instructional decisions.

Many apprentice teachers see the merit in understanding students' values and currencies and make some attempt to do so. However, their notions of what their students want or care about and what they are capable of achieving may be based on outdated, incomplete, inaccurate, or stereotypical notions rather than on a genuine understanding. They recognize that students have different abilities and values but work hard to get students to embrace a new set of "classroom values." If students reject these or otherwise do not meet expectations, apprentices may lose faith and become disillusioned. Seeking to keep students from tuning out, they may gravitate to instructional approaches that substitute entertaining students for true cognitive engagement—and they may not be able to tell the difference.

An apprentice teacher's attempt at differentiation and support is typically based on a generalized assessment of student needs. Support for struggling students tends to be general and remedial rather than proactive and individualized. Often, the teacher's intervention is too generic to make a real difference and too late to get students back on track. Apprentice teachers have a limited awareness of outside resources and thus rely heavily on school-based resources or none at all.

Apprentice teachers may confuse learning outcomes with activities, and their objectives tend to reflect both. It may not always be clear what students are expected to know and be able to do—or, what the apprentice expects students to know and be able to do is not rigorous. Although they may make some attempts at rigor, they often pitch the lesson too high or too low for students' current abilities and do not always adjust instruction to meet students where they are. In many cases, their academic expectations are low or are low for some students and high for others.

Apprentice teachers often plan lessons with the guidance of structured frameworks, but they do not always adhere to this structure during lesson delivery. Their classroom management, similarly, is uneven and inconsistent. They may show favoritism to some students while ignoring or unfairly censuring others. They may enforce some rules while letting other rules slide. They may have routines and procedures in place but fail to adhere to them consistently. As a result, transitions are awkward, provisioning is disorganized, and behavior management is inconsistent, resulting in loss of instructional time.

The climate of an apprentice's classroom is polite but not always characterized by respect. Students may not openly disrespect the teacher or each other, but they do not take responsibility for their own behavior and need to be managed by the teacher in order to be productive. Students need cues to stay on task and must be supervised closely and constantly.

Apprentice teachers have a limited repertoire of strategies and seem to apply these approaches randomly instead of thoughtfully and deliberately. As a result, even when they do the "right" thing, it is with limited effectiveness. They often score "basic," "developing," or "needs improvement" on an evaluation instrument.

Novice

Novice teaching has little to do with years of experience, although many brand-new teachers can fall into this category. Some teachers are novices because they have just started teaching and are still learning the ropes. Other novices have been teaching for some time, but they still approach teaching with a novice mindset. Either way, novice teachers tend to struggle with planning and classroom management and therefore have a disjointed approach to teaching.

When it comes to planning, novices seek rules and recipes. Their lesson objectives and essential questions are formulaic, are not written in "kid-friendly" language, and often focus on activities rather than learning outcomes. Sometimes novices rely on the objectives and activities provided by the curriculum guide without really understanding what they mean. Because they don't understand the curricular objectives, they do not know how to adapt the curriculum to meet students' needs, differentiate to provide support for struggling learners, or monitor student progress and adjust instruction accordingly.

Novices feel pressure to "get through the curriculum." They tend to plow on even in the face of student struggle and have very few strategies to address low student interest of a lack of student understanding.

Their lessons often lack coherence. The activities they plan do not match the learning objectives. They tend to jump from one activity to the next without understanding how each activity will move students toward mastery, focusing more on activity completion than on significant intellectual engagement. Novice teachers may make content-related errors or fail to catch and correct the content-related errors their students make. Even when they have a more solid grasp of the curriculum, they have a limited number of explanatory devices and a very limited range of appropriate pedagogical approaches.

Novice teachers rarely use formative assessment; their assessment is summative and focused on evaluating student performance. They may rely on tests that come with the curriculum guide, even if those tests don't match up well with their teaching practices or the learning activities throughout the unit. The assessments they create tend to focus on low-level knowledge and show little evidence of rigor. After testing, novice teachers simply record grades and move on to the next activity, missing an opportunity for using feedback to improve their own and their students' performance.

When it comes to classroom management, the novice teacher's practice is also inconsistent and ineffective. Novices' understanding of who their students are is based on generalizations and stereotypes, and they lower their expectations for learning to reflect what they believe students are capable of doing. Because they do not expect students to engage with content or be co-creators of their learning experiences, novices typically work very hard, creating a teacher-centered and teacher-directed classroom that asks little of students and can lead to exhaustion and frustration. Low expectations drive their interactions with students. They may yell at students, use sarcasm, or be insensitive or downright disrespectful—and students may counter with the same. Or teachers may be overly permissive, allowing students to run the classroom and failing to hold students accountable for poor behavior. Novice teachers struggle with establishing and enforcing routines, managing transitions, and provisioning for students. Without clear routines, they struggle to manage classroom interruptions and can easily get off track, losing a significant amount of instructional time.

Complicating matters further, novice teachers are often unaware of the resources they can use to become better teachers or to help their students become better learners. They may want to get better or may realize that they need help, but they do not know the next steps to take when it comes to improving or identifying the resources that might help them and their students. As a result, many novices feel frustrated, isolated, and hopeless. Others may be completely unaware of how ineffective they are in the classroom. Even if this is pointed out to them, they may have very little idea of how they can improve their instruction.

Novice teachers typically score as "unsatisfactory" or "needs improvement" on a teacher evaluation instrument. In observations, you may see the impulse toward doing the right thing in the classroom, but the out-come remains instruction that is inconsistent, ineffective, or incoherent.

Before You Start Diagnosing . . .

As part of a workshop series I was leading for school-based administra-tors, I introduced the skill categories of novice, apprentice, practitioner, and master teacher. After discussing why administrators might find these categories helpful, I asked the group to suggest other ways they might be used. One principal immediately raised her hand.

"I've already put all my teachers into categories," she said proudly. "At my next faculty meeting, I am going to have my teachers assess them-selves, and then I am going to meet with each one individually and com-pare my assessment with theirs. That way, they'll all know where they stand."

No.

Don't do that.

Not only had this principal skipped the whole "use real data, not gut feelings" aspect of skill diagnosis, but she also appeared to have missed the overall point of the categories. They are not about labeling or "grad-ing" or showing everyone "where they stand"; their purpose is formative rather than summative. For administrators, identifying teachers' current skill levels is necessary and important because it indicates how best to support those teachers' move toward mastery. That's why you need to use real data to help you make your assessments, not your gut feeling. That's also why you need to revisit your assessments from time to time. A teacher may start the year an apprentice, but with the right kind of sup-port, soon move to practitioner. Once a teacher makes that move, she will need a different kind of support in order to sustain her growth. You'll learn more about how to improve teaching skill in the next chapter.

YES, BUT . . .
What if teachers bristle at these labels?

It's easy to understand that a teacher who has been teaching for 20 years would not appreciate being labeled a "novice" or teachers who consider themselves master teachers would disagree with being called a "practitioner." So here's my advice on how to handle the labeling.

The first is to keep the labels to yourself. See them as for you alone—shorthand you can use to help you plan professional development or strategize your leadership approach. Again, you do not have to share these designations with teachers in order to help them, and it may actually be to your disadvantage to do so, especially when teachers do not completely trust you or the district's evaluation process.

A second option would be to adjust the category names to something that your staff might find less distressing. Sometimes using benign numbers rather than a category title (for example, having a range of 1–4 with different checkmarks for different aspects of practice) can take the sting out of assessment and put the focus on improvement in different areas. As much as no one really likes being labeled, most of us recognize it as part of workplace reality.

The third option, and my favorite, is to get teachers actively involved in the assessment and improvement process. In *Never Work Harder Than Your Students,* I include a self-assessment that helps teachers determine where they fall with regard to the four categories of teachers. When I work with schools to build teachers' mastery, as defined by the seven principles of effective instruction, the teachers take the self-assessment and work with their coaches and administrators to set goals for improvement. Even if a teacher's self-assessment is . . . *generous,* and he places himself in a category with which you do not agree, the process is still helpful, as that teacher will still be working toward improvement. The more teachers learn, the more realistic they will become about their own practice, and the more self-directed their improvement efforts are likely to be.

PRINCIPLE	NOVICE	APPRENTICE	PRACTITIONER	MASTER TEACHER
Start where your students are.	• Has a superficial understanding of who students are, based on stereotypes and generalizations. • Does not recognize that students have different values and currencies.	• Recognizes that students have different values; perception of students' currencies may be based on incomplete, inaccurate, or stereotypical notions rather than a genuine understanding of each student. • May encourage students to exchange their values for new classroom values.	• Recognizes and appreciates students' currencies but focuses on helping students acquire new currencies rather than showing them how to use the currencies they have.	• Understands self and students in terms of the currencies they value. • Negotiates and trades currencies. • Capitalizes on students' currencies.
Know where they are going.	• Provides inconsistent and incoherent instruction. • Creates lesson objectives and essential questions that are formulaic and focus on activities rather than learning outcomes. • Creates lessons that show little evidence of rigor.	• Teaches each objective separately rather than in the larger learning context. • May confuse learning outcomes with activities. • Creates lessons with unclear or unrigorous objectives. • Creates lessons that may not match students' current abilities.	• Does not align all learning activities to objectives or break them down into steps toward mastery. • Generally provides rigorous instruction focusing on helping every student master standards. • Has goals for the entire class but may not individualize these goals.	• Sets rigorous course objectives, clearly communicates these objectives to students, and breaks objectives down into steps toward mastery. • Focuses on helping students meet or exceed standards on their own. • Helps students set and meet individual goals.
Expect to get them there.	• Bases expectations on perceptions/preconceived notions of who students are and what they can do. • Demonstrates very low expectations for students.	• Sets expectations that may be too low or too low for some students and too high for others.	• Clearly communicates and maintains high expectations for most students. • May look for outside solutions rather than to students' internal resources.	• Bases expectations on own efficacy rather than on a perception of students' potential. • Shows confidence in reaching all students and communicates high expectations for ALL students.

Support them along the way.	• Takes a one-size-fits-all approach to instruction; has a limited repertoire of explanatory devices. • Uses remediation as the sole means of helping struggling students.	• Maintains a set of instructional strategies for high-level, on-level, and low-level students. • Focuses on remediation but institutes some supports within instruction.	• Plans supports that respond to students' needs throughout instruction. • Creates supports that are teacher-driven rather than student-driven.	• Proactively plans support to prevent student failure. • Anticipates and addresses confusion as a normal part of the instructional process. • Gradually releases responsibility as students learn to learn on their own.
Use feedback to help you both get better.	• Uses assessment only to evaluate performance, not as feedback. • Rarely uses test results to guide future instruction.	• Uses assessments that are generally appropriate but in a perfunctory manner. • Sets assessment goals that are not entirely clear or chooses assessment formats that don't always match well with instruction. • Uses assessment results to provide student feedback or to inform instructional decisions but on an inconsistent basis.	• Regularly uses assessment to inform instruction but does not consistently provide growth-oriented feedback to students so that they can work to improve their performance on their own.	• Uses assessment both to adjust instructional practice and to provide growth-oriented feedback to students so that they can work to improve their performance on their own.
Focus on quality, not quantity.	• Focuses on coverage and task completion versus true understanding.	• Gets through the curriculum by jettisoning some activities that do not explicitly move students toward mastery.	• Makes conscious decisions about what students need to know but attempts to teach all need-to-knows to the level of automaticity.	• Makes conscious decisions about what students need to know and how well they need to know it.
Never work harder than your students.	• Has few or inconsistent classroom routines, resulting in sloppy transitions and little to no provisioning for students. • Sets up activities and assignments; students learn passively. • Maintains a teacher-centered and teacher-directed classroom.	• Does not ask students to take responsibility for their own learning or behavior; must actively manage students to get them to be productive. • Engages students on an inconsistent basis; must provide regular cues and active supervision to keep students on task.	• Sets standards and goals for students rather than encouraging students to take complete ownership of their own learning. • May step in to rescue students when learning is challenging or uncomfortable.	• Appropriately distributes the work between self and students and sets students up to learn independently and monitor and control their own behavior. • Engages students as co-creators of their learning experiences.

3

ADDRESSING SKILL

Most teachers expand their teaching range only with carefully designed support and assistance.

—*Joseph Blase and Jo Blase,*
Handbook of Instructional Leadership

Mr. Carter was the worst teacher I have ever observed. From the moment I walked into his classroom I could feel the overwhelming boredom of both the students and Mr. Carter himself. No one seemed to want to be there. Still, when I arrived, the students were doing test corrections. For a moment, I felt hopeful. After all, just last week I had shared with the staff the value of error analysis as a way to help students clarify their thinking and deepen their learning. But then I realized that the students were doing test corrections on a true/false test. Instead of analyzing their errors, they were simply changing their incorrect "true" answers to "false" and their incorrect "false" answers to "true." They weren't even reading the test items, let alone analyzing their errors.

Later, when I asked Mr. Carter about this activity, he smiled broadly. "Ever since you told us the value of error analysis, I have wanted to try it with my students. So when I passed back their tests from last week, I asked them to do it. Aren't you proud of me?" he grinned.

"Um, well . . . I am certainly proud that you tried a new strategy," I stammered. "But what was your purpose in doing it?"

Mr. Carter looked confused. "My purpose?"

I nodded. "Yes, your purpose. What were you hoping to accomplish?"

He looked perplexed. "I just wanted to try a new strategy that you told us to do," he said.

"But *why*, Mr. Carter?"

"What do you mean *why*? I did it because you just gave us a workshop on it."

I took a breath and tried again. "In the workshop, I talked about the reasons a teacher might use error analysis. Which one of those reasons made sense for your lesson?"

Mr. Carter looked sheepish. "I don't remember those reasons, I'm sorry. But I wanted the students to do error analysis on their tests so that they would understand not to make the same errors next time."

"OK," I nodded. This was a start at least. "How did using error analysis with this true/false quiz promote that kind of understanding?"

"Look, you told us to use it in our workshop," he began. "I used it because you told us to use it."

This was going horribly wrong. I gazed at Mr. Carter, trying to figure out a way to make my point. He had used an instructional strategy without really understanding it, in a situation where it was completely inappropriate and wouldn't do his students a bit of good. I thought back to the workshop and mentally cataloged all the strategies I'd shared, the explanations of the strategies I'd shared, the tips, caveats, and practice activities. It was a good workshop. *Why wasn't he getting it?*

Only later did I realize that the problem wasn't Mr. Carter. The problem wasn't my workshop, either. The problem was that Mr. Carter wasn't ready for my workshop, which was well designed—but well designed for a teacher at a different level of skill development. For that teacher, the workshop made sense. Mr. Carter, a novice, wasn't there yet. He needed a different kind of workshop, better suited to his level of learning.

✳

Are you familiar with the 10,000-hour rule? This is the concept (first explored in Ericsson, Krampe, & Tesch-Römer, 1993; see Colvin, 2006) that it takes about 10,000 hours of deliberate practice to become great at virtually anything. What this means—and why it is so powerful and inspiring—is that what determines expertise is the amount and quality of practice, not innate talent. Just about anyone can become great at just about anything with the right kind and amount of continual practice.

If we really want to help all teachers we serve to consistently and continually improve their skill and ultimately become great teachers, we need to figure out what kind of practice each of them needs and how much. That's the problem with a one-size-fits-all approach to improving teacher skill: It doesn't work. As the example of Mr. Carter shows, each teacher needs something that is in line with where he or she is as a teacher.

Diagnosing teacher skill is the first step; it's the essential groundwork for what comes next, which is using that diagnosis to improve teacher skill. To take this second step, you need to know what good professional development looks like, specific strategies you can use to improve teacher skill, and how to match your professional development approach to the needs of the teachers you serve.

Professional Development That Leads to Mastery

Masterful teaching develops gradually and only through extensive practice. Teachers need exposure to new strategies and ways of using these strategies in the classroom, and they need time and reinforcement in order to effectively incorporate a new strategy into their repertoire. By providing professional development focused on both the right kind of learning for each teacher and the right kind of practice, you can refine and improve the skill of every member of your instructional staff, which includes their "teacher sense"—that internal, principle-based guide that they need to make good decisions. Well-structured practice helps teachers at every skill level perceive more, know more, and remember more. Professional growth follows a predictable pattern: It becomes a cycle. Increased practice increases skill; increased skill fuels the drive to increase practice.

Fortunately for us, there has been a lot of research conducted about what the right kind of practice looks like (Colvin, 2008; Coyle, 2009). That research confirms for us that if we really want to improve teacher skill, we need to provide practice that is differentiated, deliberate, and developmental.

Differentiated Practice

Teachers at different stages of skill development need different types of support in order to move them to the next stage. Supports that help novice and apprentice teachers may not help (and may even hurt) practitioners and master teachers. The best way to increase a teacher's skill is to do so incrementally, always working within—but at the outer edge of—a teacher's current abilities. As Figure 3.1 shows, you have to develop a novice teacher differently than you do a master teacher because they have different needs.

Figure 3.1   Professional Growth Needs by Skill-Level Category

Skill Level	Primary Characteristics	Professional Growth Need
Novice	• Has minimal exposure/experience/ expertise.	Needs to acquire a concrete understanding of what it takes to be a good teacher.
Apprentice	• Is building expertise but still needs supervision. • Can perform some more routine tasks independently.	Needs to internalize the standards and principles of effective teaching in order to become an independent problem solver and develop "teacher sense."
Practitioner	• Makes accurate and reliable judgments and monitors the effect these judgments have on students. • Shows both skill and economy in teaching practice. • Can teach others.	Needs help integrating skills into a seamless performance and developing adaptive expertise.
Master Teacher	• Can deal with unusual and tough cases. • Exemplifies best practices, standards, regulations, or ideals. • Practice is seamless.	Needs help remaining mindful in his or her practice.

Deliberate Practice

There is a difference between general professional development and deliberate practice. General professional development is rather like throwing a pot of pasta against a wall and seeing what sticks: improvement is random and left mainly to chance. Even if it "sticks," it will never move teachers beyond a plateau of acceptable performance because it mostly involves going through the motions over and over again. Deliberate practice, by contrast, is designed to improve *specifics* of a teacher's performance. Deliberate practice concentrates on critical aspects of a teacher's performance and helps teachers gradually refine performance through repetition after feedback. If it is highly targeted, individualized, and intentional, it will improve expertise over time.

To foster deliberate practice, identify certain sharply defined elements of performance that need to be improved and then help teachers concentrate on those areas. You could identify a certain principle of effective instruction (such as "know where your students are going"), a specific subdomain on your evaluation instrument, or a specific teaching skill as part of a schoolwide initiative. Identify clear goals rather than ill-defined areas of improvement. Then ensure teachers have the time and opportunities to repeat specific teaching skills over and over until these become their natural response to students.

Developmental Practice

If you are going to improve teacher skill, you have to stretch teachers just beyond their current level of performance. One of the reasons that I separate teacher skill into four distinct categories is to clearly delineate each level of performance. You don't want to stretch teachers too far. If the challenge is too hard, they will become frustrated and give up. If the challenge is too easy, however, they will become bored and stop trying. The key is to design practice activities that help teachers stretch beyond their current abilities but not so far that success feels completely out of reach. Begin by providing teachers with goals that are initially just outside of their current ability yet can be mastered, with practice, within a short time. The idea is to move teachers to the next level of mastery rather than to total mastery. Thus, you stretch novices to the level of apprentice, apprentices to the level of practitioner, practitioners to mastery, and master teachers to greater mastery. Teachers should focus on the next step, not the final destination.

So, every teacher requires differentiated, deliberate, and developmental practice—but how do you start? One way "in" is to look at eight essential professional development approaches that benefit teachers at all levels—namely, opportunities for *evaluation, elaboration, observation, practice, feedback, coaching, collaboration,* and *reflection* (see Figure 3.2). In the pages to come, we'll look at how to tailor these eight approaches to skill development for teachers at all levels, from novice to master teacher.

 **Tools to Use**

For strategies that will help you meet management challenges, see **Tools 5, 6,** and **7** in the Appendix.

Yes, this kind of instructional leadership does take time, and it does require careful and sometimes creative organization and time management. However, if being a great school leader means never underestimating your teachers, it also means never underestimating *yourself* and what you and your teachers can accomplish together.

Building Skill in Novice Teachers

Novice teachers struggle because they have a very limited understanding of what masterful teaching entails and do not have effective strategies for helping students learn. They may lack a basic understanding of teaching in general (or their subject or grade level in particular) and need to *acquire* practical knowledge of good teaching before they can improve.

When working with novice teachers, your goal is to simply help them acquire the skills, strategies, and ways of thinking about instruction that ultimately will help them become master teachers. Novice teachers benefit from a directive approach that provides information in small chunks and offers frequent practice opportunities. Focus on helping them learn the principles of effective instruction rather than acquiring a bunch of specific strategies. It can be tempting to try to help them learn a new strategy or technique in order to quickly improve their instructional practice, but doing so neglects laying the important foundation that ultimately leads to real mastery. Instead of inundating them with strategies, help novice teachers acquire solid foundational knowledge in three key areas:

Figure 3.2   Eight Strategies to Support Skill Development

Provide Opportunities For . . .	Why?
Evaluation	All teachers need opportunities both to self-evaluate and to receive evaluative feedback. This gives them a chance to see what they are doing well, identify goals for improvement, and detect holes in their practice that need to be addressed.
Elaboration	Teachers need a chance to think critically about effective teaching, discuss best practices, and deepen their understanding of effective pedagogy. Worked examples, case studies, and facilitated discussions can improve teachers' understanding of what is required and expected of them, which they can then apply to their own practice.
Observation	Peer observation is critical for expanding teachers' repertoire of skills and helping them think critically about their practice. Teachers need to see examples and nonexamples of effective practice. Walk-throughs, observations and discussions, and giving and receiving peer feedback not only provide teachers exemplars of good practice; they help teachers think critically about what works and doesn't work in their own classroom.
Practice	If teachers are going to improve, they need a chance to practice and refine their skills in a nonevaluative environment. This includes setting and monitoring goals, rehearsing teaching tasks, reflecting on what they are doing, and collecting feedback. Teachers can collect feedback from students, examine changes in student data, or seek feedback from other colleagues.
Feedback	Formal feedback lets teachers know how well they are progressing toward their goals. Providing teachers with feedback specific to their goals helps them refine their practice, identify opportunities for growth, and monitor the effectiveness of their growth process.
Coaching	Providing teachers with subject-specific or curriculum-based coaching can help them quickly acquire expertise. Coaching can come from a colleague, a district-based instructional coach, a curriculum specialist in the district, or an outside expert.
Collaboration	Teachers often learn best from other teachers. Pairing or grouping teachers to coplan, co-teach, and provide peer feedback allows them to learn from one another.
Reflection	Engaging teachers in reflective conversations, providing professional development opportunities that foster reflection, and modeling reflection can help teachers examine their practice, set or refine goals, and ultimately improve their teaching.

knowledge for practice, knowledge in practice, and knowledge of practice (Yendol-Hoppey & Dana, 2010).

Knowledge for practice has to do with teaching technique and strategy. Novice teachers need to learn how to mindfully implement specific research-based instructional strategies and how to effectively and efficiently manage a classroom. To help them acquire knowledge for practice, root any strategy, technique, or approach in one or more of the seven principles of effective instruction (Jackson, 2009; see Chapter 2). This provides novice teachers with a practical framework for understanding teaching in general and their own teaching in particular. This also has the benefit of preventing cognitive overload; novice teachers can become overwhelmed by how much they have to learn.

Knowledge in practice is providing novice teachers opportunities to implement the principles and strategies they are learning in the classroom setting and to reflect on the resulting effect on students. Nonevaluative observers can provide feedback on how well they have implemented the strategy. Engaging in reflective conversations (What is the teacher learning through implementing the strategy?) and providing coaching can help novice teachers implement strategies or principles more effectively.

Knowledge of practice is the basis for becoming a reflective practitioner. Master teachers know how to think critically about their own practice and observe and learn from the practice of other teachers. Novice teachers need to learn how to reflect—not just reflect on the effectiveness of a particular strategy or principle but also reflect on how to take individual teaching strategies and principles and place them in context for their entire teaching practice.

Evaluation

Evaluations show teachers where they stand and can spur them toward improved performance. However, novice teachers tend to perform poorly on formal evaluations. They may be unsure of the standards and generally do not have the skills to meet the standards.

Take time to explain the standards to novice teachers; provide them with examples of behaviors that differentiate unsatisfactory performance from satisfactory performance. For example, Domain 2 of the Danielson rubric (used by many districts as their teacher evaluation system) separates "unsatisfactory" from "basic" classroom management performance on the basis of the existence of standards of conduct (2011, p. 42). Thus, if novice teachers want to improve in this area, they can establish and attempt to enforce standards of conduct. Identifying *one thing* novice teachers can do to move from unsatisfactory to satisfactory (even if that is still low on the evaluation instrument) will help them set goals that are concrete and within their reach.

Elaboration

Help novice teachers learn new skills by providing them with *worked examples*—step-by-step demonstrations of how to solve a problem or complete a task—such as exemplars of lesson plans, model assessments and assignments, and model instructional techniques. Explain each step, discuss the principles that make the worked example effective, and then ask the novice teacher to articulate the steps and the principles involved.

The value of worked examples is twofold: there is value in seeing, step by step, how to do something important, and engaging novice teachers in a conversation about the worked example (and having them explain why the choices were made) helps them learn the principles of effective teaching. By providing worked examples, you not only show novice teachers the desired result, you also show them how they can achieve that desired result themselves.

Observation

One of my favorite ways to help novice teachers build skill both quickly and mindfully is for them to observe other teachers on walk-throughs (for the walk-through protocol I use, see Jackson, 2008).

Start by identifying one skill that you want novice teachers to acquire. Then, select three to five teachers for observation; plan to spend about five minutes in each classroom specifically observing for that skill. Don't stack the deck, here: Choose teachers with varying abilities so that novice teachers can see a range of performance. This will help them begin to discriminate between effective and ineffective practice and make connections to their own practice. Immediately after the walk-through, meet with the novice teacher and facilitate a discussion of what worked and what didn't work, and help draw connections to the teacher's own practice.

Practice

Novice teachers tend to focus on practicing superficial behaviors rather than on deep practice. Identify one or two key behaviors that will make the biggest difference to their teaching; have them practice these and give them lots of feedback on what is working and what tweaks they need to make.

For instance, one novice teacher we worked with, Claire, really struggled with classroom management. After observing her class, we realized that the root cause of many of her classroom management issues was that she did not script transitions. Her students seized upon these opportunities to talk to their friends, get up and sharpen their pencils, or play around with the items in their desks. Claire learned to script her transitions, including what she would say, what supplies she would direct her students to retrieve, and so on—and then she practiced these transitions over and over until they became natural. Her classroom management improved dramatically, and this gave her the confidence to address other issues in her practice.

Feedback

Providing novice teachers with a lot of feedback pointing out everything that needs to be addressed will overwhelm them and guarantee that they will either make superficial changes or shut down and make no change at all. Novice teachers need *diagnostic feedback* that identifies the root problem: tell them what you observed and why it isn't working. Identify one thing they can do right now to dramatically improve their practice, and focus your feedback on that. The more concrete that one thing is, the better.

Coaching

So much of a novice teacher's practice needs improvement that it is tempting to rush in and give advice on everything that isn't working. This is a mistake. Focus coaching on one or two key areas; resist the temptation to rewrite lesson plans or tell novice teachers how you would do something. Instead, spend time diagnosing the root cause of a specific difficulty and discuss the principle of teaching involved. Provide novice teachers with general strategies and help them shape those strategies into something that works for who they are and who their students are. Otherwise, novice teachers will simply do what you've told them to do or try to teach just like you—what Allison Zmuda has called "doing bad karaoke"—and never learn how to think on their own.

Collaboration

Novice teachers need opportunities to learn from their colleagues through collaboration, but they may feel intimidated or that they have nothing to offer. Give novice teachers opportunities to collaborate with colleagues during planning, but be careful about pairing them with master teachers. Master teachers' practice is so fluid and natural that it may appear magical to a novice. Also, master teachers have become so adept at teaching that they may have trouble articulating why they do what they do or explaining a strategy or approach in terms a novice can understand. It is better to pair novices with practitioners. Practitioners have become really proficient at teaching, but because they are still refining particular aspects of their practice, they are able to articulate why they make decisions and can explain how to perform a particular teaching behavior.

Reflection

Novice teachers don't tend to be highly reflective. They need help understanding why reflection is important and how to reflect in a way that will improve their practice. At this stage, reflection will need to be concrete. Give them something specific on which to reflect and time for them to focus on reflection. For example, ask them to try a new instructional practice and later spend 5 or 10 minutes asking them how it worked and what differences they noticed in the way their students behaved when the new practice was in use. Ask them what felt comfortable and what felt uncomfortable and why. This will deepen their practice of the specific behavior and cultivate a general reflective approach to teaching.

Checkpoint Summary

Develop novice teachers' basic teaching proficiency by helping them **acquire** *knowledge of, in, and for practice.*

TOOLS FOR SKILL DEVELOPMENT	CHARACTERIZED BY	RESULTING IN
Evaluation	Moving from unsatisfactory to satisfactory or basic; realistic goal setting	A concrete understanding of how to improve and achievable goals that improve practice
Elaboration	Worked examples	An understanding of how to improve teaching and work through teaching challenges
Observation	Walk-throughs	An understanding of what works and doesn't work and how specific practices affect students
Practice	A focus on specific skills	Growth in specific teaching behaviors
Feedback	Diagnostic feedback	A better understanding of the root causes of ineffective teaching
Coaching	A focus on one or two key areas	Reduced cognitive overload
Collaboration	Working with practitioners	A better understanding of the thought process behind good teaching
Reflection	Concrete examples	A new, more reflective approach to teaching and more teaching coherence

Building Skill in Apprentice Teachers

Apprentice teachers struggle because, although they have some understanding of what it takes to be effective in the classroom, their application of strategies and techniques is inconsistent, making their teaching scattered. They need help using principles of effective instruction so that they can better recognize and solve classroom and learning problems and develop a more coherent, harmonious, and productive approach to teaching.

Apprentices have already acquired an understanding of the mastery principles and recognize areas in their own teaching where they could make improvements. They may have even started experimenting with some of the principles but are still not sure how to consistently apply them. In their attempts to apply the principles perfectly, they can become overwhelmed—and their practice gets even more disjointed.

To make the most of their practice, help apprentices select one or two principles at a time to work on and *apply* to their teaching. Once they become more comfortable practicing those principles, they can begin to add others to their practice. The goal is to help apprentices develop a "teacher sense," their own internal voice, where they become less reliant on formulas and prescriptions and more confident solving problems independently.

Evaluation

Apprentices are on the edge of being good at teaching. As with novices, explain to apprentices the difference between satisfactory performance and good performance on your evaluation instrument—but your goal for apprentices is to help them internalize these standards. They need to be clear about what makes an effective teacher. Rather than focusing on specific behaviors, use the evaluation process to help apprentices understand how individual teaching behaviors work together to make teaching effective. Help them focus on the overall principle, domain, or teaching standard so that they can begin to internalize what good teaching really is. For their next evaluation, help them set goals for improving in a particular domain or standard rather than for specific indicators.

Elaboration

One of the fastest ways to help apprentices learn how to think like practitioners and master teachers is to present them with specific classroom-based case studies and work with them to solve particular challenges. Give teachers a case study, and ask them how they would address the teaching challenge it presents. Discuss why the strategy they have chosen might or might not work, and identify the principle or principles of effective teaching involved.

Try to give apprentices several case studies that involve each principle and help them see the through-lines across case studies so that they can begin to detect patterns, uncover subtle differences, and start to develop schema for how to effectively solve problems in the classroom.

Observation

Apprentices often know what they should be doing and understand the supporting principle on an intellectual level. However, because they may not know what effective practice of the principle looks like, they need to see it in action. Take them on walk-throughs of classrooms or show videos of model lessons, choosing for your examples both situations in which the teacher is particularly adept at practicing a principle and ones where the principle is largely absent; help them see the difference. Show them model lessons on the individual skills they are attempting to develop so that they can see what effective practice looks like. After walk-throughs, video examples, or model lessons, be sure to engage apprentices in reflective conversations to help them articulate what they observed and identify ways to apply their new knowledge to their own practice.

Practice

Apprentices should be practicing principles rather than individual behaviors. A principle incorporates several behaviors and is focused on the overall impact on students. Isolate one principle (or two at the most) that will have the biggest impact on their practice, and break down the principle into its key dispositions and behaviors. Then have the apprentice practice this principle. This helps the apprentice teacher to begin to look at teaching as more than a set of behaviors and to start to internalize the principles of effective instruction.

Feedback

The point of providing feedback to apprentices is to develop their internal "teacher sense" to guide their practice. Apprentices need feedback that is prescriptive: Tell them what you observed as well as how they can improve in their practice of a specific principle. Don't overwhelm them with a laundry list of suggestions. Too many instructional leaders try to rewrite teachers' lesson plans or give teachers an entirely different direction for their instruction. That is not feedback; that's taking over. Instead, focus on what you actually observe in their practice and offer possible solutions for correcting what did not work. Don't give them a new lesson; show them how they could deliver that same lesson better through more effective application of the targeted principle.

Coaching

Coaching should focus on how individual teaching behaviors embody a principle. Your goal is to give apprentices the most important information about their practice and suggestions for strategies that will enhance what they are already doing and will fit into their style of teaching. Be careful here. There is a real danger of being overly prescriptive and taking over their practice. You don't want to do the work for them. To avoid being overly prescriptive, always give apprentices two options and then let them choose which option would work best. This models good decision making and maintains the apprentices' ownership over their own practice.

Collaboration

Apprentices need two types of collaboration: They need to be able to contribute, and they need opportunities to learn from other teachers. Give apprentices a chance to share procedural information with novice teachers. Apprentices still remember what it was like to be a novice and can anticipate questions, areas of confusion, and sources of frustration. This also helps cultivate leadership in apprentice teachers and gives them opportunities to articulate what they are learning. Help apprentices learn from other teachers by grouping them with practitioner or master teachers who are particularly adept at practicing the principle the apprentices are attempting to master. This enables them to "look behind the veil" and glimpse the decision-making process practitioners and master teachers use—and to begin to internalize this process in their own practice.

Reflection

In the course of practicing a particular principle of effective teaching, apprentices may get so mired in the details that they lose sight of the principle itself. Thus, it is important to shape reflective conversations around the principle. Help apprentices think about the importance of the principle, how individual teaching behaviors support or detract from their practice of the principle, and how they can continue to improve in their practice of the principle. Ask reflective questions to spark thinking; when apprentices start to articulate thinking, paraphrase their comments so that they can hear, process, and internalize their developing understanding of the principles. (For a planning tool to help you prepare for these conversations, see Jackson, 2008.)

 Checkpoint Summary

*Develop apprentices' ability to **apply** the principles of effective instruction in their own practice (their "teaching sense") by helping them internalize the principles and recognize the difference between satisfactory and effective performance.*

TOOLS FOR SKILL DEVELOPMENT	CHARACTERIZED BY	RESULTING IN
Evaluation	A focus on the domains of effective teaching	An internalization of the standards and a better understanding of how individual behaviors come together to make teaching effective
Elaboration	Case studies	A personal schema of effective teaching and a process for good decision making

TOOLS FOR SKILL DEVELOPMENT	CHARACTERIZED BY	RESULTING IN
Observation	Walk-throughs and model lessons	A personal schema of what effective teaching looks like
Practice	Practice of individual principles of effective instruction	New proficiency in the principles
Feedback	Prescriptive feedback	A refinement of individual skills
Coaching	Suggestions based on the principles of effective instruction	Improved decision making in the classroom
Collaboration	Opportunities to contribute and opportunities to learn	The emergence of leadership abilities and new learning from master teachers
Reflection	Conversations around the principles of effective instruction	Internalization of the principles of effective instruction

Building Skill in Practitioners

Although practitioner teachers have successfully acquired a range of teaching strategies and skills, they have not yet integrated them seamlessly into their teaching practice. As a result, practitioners still have areas of their practice that need refining in order for them to become master teachers.

The distinction between a practitioner and a master teacher is the difference between routine expertise and adaptive expertise. Practitioners have routine expertise; they are very effective at solving problems that are typical, routine, and expected. They are less adept at adapting to new problems, especially if those new problems cannot be solved by their current skills set. Master teachers have adaptive expertise; they are very good at solving problems that are novel, unusual, and unfamiliar. They have learned to constantly evolve in order to develop new skills as warranted by new and unfamiliar contexts. Master teachers know how to revise their existing problem-solving strategies (or assemble new ones) to face new challenges or problems. Thus, the goal for moving practitioners to mastery is really to help them learn how to develop adaptive expertise.

Evaluation

Practitioners are not in danger of losing their jobs, and being "good enough" may well be good enough for them. We complicate this problem of complacency by making mastery so elite that it is generally accepted that most teachers never get there. In fact, many school districts discourage observers from rating teachers in the highest category even if their teaching merits it. It's as if we want to keep masterful teaching rarified instead of building a school culture where it is legitimately ubiquitous.

As I've stated, teaching at the master level is not just possible; it's probable, with the right kind of effort. To help practitioners move in that direction, it is critical to demystify masterful teaching and make it a goal for every practitioner. The difference between master teachers and practitioners is subtle but important: It is the difference between helping students learn effectively and helping students learn effectively *on their own*. Use the evaluation process to help practitioners understand that subtle difference and how they can move toward mastery.

Elaboration

Opportunities for elaboration highlight for practitioners the subtle differences between practitioner- and master-level teaching. Guide teachers at the practitioner level toward action research, which gives them a chance to refine their teaching practice in ways that further support students becoming independent thinkers and learners. Then help examine the results of these efforts. Action research promotes the development of adaptive expertise by providing practitioners with a systematic way to articulate a problem, formulate an approach to solving the problem, and most importantly, revise that approach as they encounter unforeseen challenges or receive unexpected data that reveal that their approach isn't working (Yendol-Hoppey & Dana, 2010).

Observation

Because practitioners are working on refining their own practice, they benefit from observing themselves as much as they benefit from observing others. Although you should continue to engage practitioners in occasional walk-throughs, spend more time helping them objectively observe their own teaching. Ask them to record a segment of a lesson and then watch the recording alone, with a peer, or with you to study specific aspects of their practice. As you watch the recording together, stop it every so often to discuss what is happening and to offer feedback. Rather than nitpick individual behaviors, note how well several teaching moves and principles are integrated. Focus attention on both what they are doing and the effect their decisions have on students. Ask practitioners to identify alternate ways of handling specific teaching situations. The objectivity and distance they get from observing their recorded lessons will help them explore additional strategies or look for ways to adapt their practice to better meet students' needs.

Practice

Practitioners need opportunities to refine their practice. They need *micropractice*—to repeat effective teaching behaviors over and over again until these become unconscious and natural. Focus practice not on individual skills but on integrating two or more skills. For instance, if a teacher who is really great at questioning strategies has been working on giving students growth-oriented feedback, have the teacher integrate these two skills so that the questioning process also provides students effective growth-oriented feedback on their responses. Or perhaps you have a teacher who is good at understanding students' currencies and also effective at helping students take ownership over their own learning. Help that teacher integrate these two skills so that students are empowered to take ownership over their own learning in ways that honor their preferred currencies.

Feedback

The danger with practitioners is not too little feedback but too much. Too much feedback at this stage of their practice will hinder the development of independent thought and decision making. Practitioners need *summary feedback*, which tells them how they are performing overall and highlights general tendencies in their performance. This leaves room for practitioners to fill in the blanks themselves and adjust or adapt their practice to better meet students' needs.

Coaching

Practitioners need opportunities to develop skill independently. Only when they appear to be at a dead end in their search for solutions or stop and ask for your help should you offer coaching. This pushes practitioners to do their own problem solving, helps them attend to their own internal feedback, and allows them the space to adapt their practice. When they do need coaching, focus on helping them to synthesize their current practice rather than develop new skills or strategies. Practitioners have a fine repertoire of skills and strategies; coaching should help them refine what they do well already and integrate their skills until their practice becomes seamless.

Collaboration

Practitioners need to collaborate with both other practitioners and master teachers, and also with novices and apprentices. Collaborating with practitioners and master teachers helps them think critically about their practice, learn from their colleagues, and identify new ways of solving problems. Collaborating with novices and apprentices provides them with teacher leadership opportunities. In teaching others what they know, they also refine their own practice and, in the process, learn more about why they do what they do.

Reflection

Practitioners need reflection to help them better attend to their "inner teacher" and evaluate their performance in terms of its effect on student learning. Because you want them to think through their errors and come up with possible solutions, you will have to tolerate a fair amount of silence and floundering at first. Use reflective questions to prompt this kind of thinking but resist jumping in and offering feedback. Instead, help practitioners work through their challenges on their own.

📋 Checkpoint Summary

*Develop practitioners' adaptive expertise by helping them **assimilate** the principles of effective instruction into all aspects of practice.*

TOOLS FOR SKILL DEVELOPMENT	CHARACTERIZED BY	RESULTING IN
Evaluation	A focus on the nuanced differences between proficient and mastery performance	The demystification of mastery and revision of it as a concrete and attainable goal
Elaboration	Action research	The development of adaptive expertise rooted in real data
Observation	Self-recorded classroom lessons	Objective reflection on practice and specific problem solving
Practice	Micropractice	Skill refinement until behaviors become unconscious and seamless
Feedback	A summative focus: What performance looks like overall	Better integration of skills and principles
Coaching	Independence	Self-directed practice improvement and the development of adaptive expertise
Collaboration	Peer-to-peer interaction and teacher leadership opportunities with novices	Critical thinking about their own practice and further self-directed practice refinement
Reflection	Reflective questioning and silence	More attention paid to the "inner teacher"

Building Skill in Master Teachers

The challenge for master teachers is how to maintain their effectiveness over the long term. Master teachers' strength is that their teaching is seamless and automatic. But if they are not careful, this strength can also be their curse. If their practice becomes too automatic, then it also becomes mindless. Thus, master teachers need leadership that helps them be deliberately mindful about how they practice their teaching craft, or they are in danger of stagnating.

Master teachers may struggle differently than other teachers, but they still struggle. Because they have mastered their craft, they can sometimes become inflexible, insisting that their way is the right way, even the only way, to approach a challenge. Another pitfall for master teachers is that, because they are so used to seeing the world in a particular way, they can tend to base classroom decisions on their extensive past experience rather than the unique needs of the students in front of them.

By keeping master teachers mindful, you help them continue to grow, innovate, and reflect on their practice. This keeps their practice fresh and ever-evolving, and it keeps master teachers actively engaged in their own practice and in the school community.

Evaluation

Many master teachers do not see the evaluation process as particularly informative. It is just another hurdle they have to jump in order to be free to do the job they love. This attitude is understandable. By the time they reach mastery, the observation process is either a rubber stamp on a job well done or downright maddening if the observer feels compelled to provide some sort of feedback for improvement or downgrade in points in order to justify the need for evaluation.

The evaluation process can be used to help maintain mastery for master teachers by identifying specifically what makes the master teacher so effective. Remind master teachers of the specific choices they have made that have led to mastery and which make them particularly effective. Use the evaluation process as an opportunity to present even more challenge to the master teacher by identifying opportunities to tweak performance, if for no other reason than to avoid stagnation. One of the dangers of mastery performance is that, after a while, master teachers lose the ability to see themselves objectively. The evaluation process is the perfect opportunity to hold up a mirror to master teachers and offer them an objective view of their performance. This is why people like Itzhak Perlman and Tiger Woods—who appear to have reached the peak of their professions—still submit to coaching. They need an objective observer to help them see and hear themselves. They need that objectivity to stay at the top of their game. The evaluation process provides the master teacher with that objectivity.

Elaboration

Teaching for the master teacher is automatic and natural. But, over time, it can become a rote response to students. To keep their teaching muscles fresh and engaged, provide master teachers with opportunities to participate in problem-solving activities. Present them with real problems that you or other teachers are currently facing with students. The more complex and involved the problem, the better. Engage them in a discussion of the problem, ask them to pinpoint possible root causes, and brainstorm and vet possible solutions. Doing so helps master teachers stretch their teaching muscles, piques their interest, reminds them of the reasons why they make certain teaching choices, and puts them in a situation where they have to be creative in their pursuit of solutions.

Observation

Master teachers benefit from peer visits with reflection, a process that involves the master teacher inviting a peer (in most cases, another master teacher) to observe a specific aspect of teaching practice, so together they may reflect on the teaching and learning taking place. Rather than asking a colleague to observe and give general feedback, the master teacher chooses a focus that will help meet a particular learning goal. Peer visits are a mutual process in which the master teacher is both observed and has an opportunity to observe another teacher. Following the peer visit, both teachers engage in a reflective conversation, in which the teacher, not the observer, does the majority of the talking. These conversations promote authentic professional examination of teaching practices among colleagues in an atmosphere of mutual support and trust, and perpetuate the belief in the necessity of constant learning and improvement.

Practice

Master teachers do not need to rehearse the same skills over and over; they need to continue to be more mindful as they teach. A skill, once gained, feels utterly natural, as if you've always possessed it. The more you use a skill, the less aware you become of using it. The benefit of this automaticity is that teaching for master teachers is a lot less effortful. But because their teaching is automatic, it may not be as thoughtful. Practice helps the master teacher remain conscious and deliberate.

Offer master teachers practice that involves some form of innovation. They tend to become really frustrated with professional development that covers skills they already know. Master teachers want more challenge and a chance to be creative. Give them opportunities to come up with new approaches and ways of achieving results . . . and then give them room to try their innovations, collect data, and refine their ideas. Once their innovations have been worked out, they will likely become standard practice throughout the school and not only improve the master teachers' practice but also make a significant difference in the effectiveness of all the teachers in the school.

Feedback

Master teachers really benefit from precise feedback. Whereas with novice and apprentice teachers the frequency of feedback is what is important, and practitioners need summary feedback, master teachers need very precise information to help them fine-tune their practice. Rather than telling them that several of their students "seemed lost" during a lesson, note that three students began to fiddle with their papers right at the point where the teacher made an offhand reference to a recent performance of Shakespeare's *Twelfth Night*. This kind of specific feedback helps master teachers to pinpoint areas in their practice that need to be addressed and the exact tweak they need to make to improve.

Coaching

The kind of specialized coaching that would benefit master teachers is likely to be beyond the skill set of any other coach or leader in your building. Give master teachers the coaching that is relevant to them by paying for them to attend special workshops and providing them with books and other resources by experts in the field. Ask them to lead professional development for other teachers after they have digested and operationalized what they have learned.

Collaboration

Give master teachers the opportunity to collaborate with teachers of lesser skill so that they can have the chance to explain the thinking behind their instructional decisions. Explaining how they apply the principles of effective instruction to their own craft will further refine their understanding of the principles and help them be more reflective about how they will apply the principles in the future. However, master teachers also need plenty of time to work alone or with self-selected colleagues so that they can innovate and come up with new strategies. Balance collaboration with individual work so that you do not frustrate master teachers.

Reflection

Master teachers struggle with articulating why they are so effective or explaining the choices they make. Effective teaching feels so natural to them that it seems as if it is the most obvious response to students' needs. The goal of reflection for master teachers is to help them articulate their thinking and the effect of their choices on students. Help them consider their teaching choices; discover alternate strategies; become more open to new ideas and approaches; analyze their decision making; weigh competing points of view; examine their personal goals; and unearth commonalities, patterns, differences, and interrelations in their teaching attitudes and behaviors. Doing so helps them refine their practice and remain mindful about it.

Back to Mr. Carter

The conversation I had with Mr. Carter kept me up much of that night. How could I get through to him? I mulled over and ultimately rejected every professional development and coaching trick I knew at the time. Nothing seemed like it would work. *Maybe,* I thought, *Mr. Carter just shouldn't be a teacher.*

But a nagging voice in the back of my mind wouldn't let me settle on that. *Any teacher*, it insisted. The next morning as I drove to the school, it occurred to me that if Mr. Carter were one of my students in high school, struggling to grasp a concept, I would have used a much different approach. That proved to make the difference.

Checkpoint Summary

*Help master teachers remain mindful in their practice by encouraging them to **adapt** their skills and the principles of effective instruction to new, novel, or unpredictable situations.*

TOOLS FOR SKILL DEVELOPMENT	CHARACTERIZED BY	RESULTING IN
Evaluation	Challenge and reflection	Increased objectivity and heightened purpose
Elaboration	Problem solving	More creativity and mindfulness
Observation	Peer visits with reflection	Increased objectivity and more mindfulness
Practice	Innovation	The establishment of new best practices, standards, and ideals
Feedback	Precision	Pinpointed areas for improvement
Coaching	Master classes and access to experts	More innovation and further skill refinement
Collaboration	A balance of collaboration and opportunities to work alone	Opportunities to articulate their thinking and consider new perspectives
Reflection	Articulating the thinking behind their practice	More mindful practice

In helping Mr. Carter build his skill, I first had to realize that he was a novice. I had been treating him like a practitioner, assuming that he was ready to incorporate new strategies into his practice, when in reality he needed help with the basics. Next, I had to adjust my attitude. I had to persist with Mr. Carter in the same way that I would persist with a struggling student who didn't understand something that I was teaching. So I focused on helping Mr. Carter understand on a theoretical level that everything he did in the classroom needed an instructional purpose and should fit in with his learning goals. I worked on helping Mr. Carter articulate his learning goals. I worked to help Mr. Carter learn how to plan more effectively.

Did it work? Did Mr. Carter somehow magically transform from the worst teacher I have ever observed into the best teacher I have ever seen?

Well, no. Or, rather, *not yet*. Mr. Carter still has a long way to go. But he is now slowly moving toward mastery. He is making progress in areas where he was stalled. Mr. Carter understands just how and why his teaching isn't working, and he has a concrete plan to improve.

About Mandated "Improvement Plans"

Improving skill isn't magical. It requires a lot of hard work. It takes time. But if you want to put all of your teachers on the path to mastery, improving skill this way meets all of your teachers where they are while also helping all of your teachers access professional development that directly addresses their individual needs.

It would be hard to design a more potent way to discourage teachers from improving than the improvement plans that are currently in place in most school systems. These plans seem not only to focus on surface features of a teacher's performance but also to be designed more as a way to meet paperwork requirements than actually to help teachers advance toward mastery. They foster compliance rather than cooperation, and they violate everything we know about genuine growth and development. As a result, most improvement plans are almost guaranteed to fail.

 **Tools to Use**

See **Tools 4 and 5** in the Appendix for a professional development planning template and suggested ways to track teachers' progress.

Still, many districts require improvement plans as a part of the process of addressing substandard teaching. If you must use an improvement plan, use one that is focused on supporting and building better teaching, grounded in the principles and professional development approaches outlined in this chapter. Any "improvement plan" should target the specific root causes for a teacher's ineffectiveness and offer developmental, deliberate, and differentiated practice and support (see Figure 3.3).

Figure 3.3 A Targeted Plan for Professional Development

Goal: *(What do you hope to accomplish with this plan?)*		
• Help Mrs. Lemons better manage her classroom. ☑ Increased time on task for students ☑ Decreased interruptions ☑ De-escalation of classroom conflicts		

Opportunities for Professional Development *(Include dates/frequency)*	Characterized By *(What steps will you take?)*	Resulting In *(How will you know if it is working?)*
Evaluation Formal: 10/17 and 4/30 Informal: 12/14 and 2/22	Point out specific actions she can take in the target domain and show her the difference between Unsatisfactory and Satisfactory. Include her in setting goals above using language from the evaluation instrument.	Mrs. Lemons will set one improvement goal using the language of the target domain. The goal will represent a clear move from Needs Improvement to Satisfactory.
Elaboration 10/30	Give worked examples of teachers who de-escalate classroom conflicts. Use Levin and Nolan's *Principles of Classroom Management* (2009) for examples.	Written reflections on worked examples demonstrating an understanding of process.
Observation 11/10, 11/30, 1/15	Take on walk-throughs focused on classroom management. Develop clear look-fors.	Application to her own classroom.
Practice Ongoing	Focus on starting class on time, transitions, provisioning, and monitoring behavior.	Increased proficiency (moving from Needs Improvement to Satisfactory) in key classroom management skills.
Feedback Weekly	Weekly 15-minute observations by instructional coach or administrator, with targeted diagnostic feedback.	Can articulate the root causes of classroom disruptions. Ability to prevent classroom disruptions during observations.
Coaching Biweekly	Coaching on specific classroom management strategies based on feedback.	Increased proficiency in classroom management strategies (from Needs Improvement to Satisfactory).
Collaboration 10/30–11/16	Work with Ms. Tran on planning major project to help with provisioning and planning.	Major project will be planned to reduce disruptions due to provisioning.
Reflection Preconference 10/15, 4/28 12/12, 2/20 Post-conference 10/18, 5/1 12/15, 2/23	Reflect on growth in identified growth areas. Do a self-evaluation.	Track growth and increased proficiency in key areas.

YES, BUT . . .
Don't teachers need improvement plans in order to get better?

The typical solution to ineffective teaching is to put the teacher on a learning plan, which identifies the teaching behavior or behaviors that must change, establishes criteria for improvement, includes some sort of accountability measure, outlines supports that will be made available, and determines a time line for when improvement must be made. It is a tidy bit of paperwork, but does it really result in a lasting improvement in the way a teacher thinks or, more important, how students perform?

Not really. In most cases, teachers who want to hold onto their jobs comply with the plan. They attempt to do everything the plan outlines, dotting every *i* and crossing every *t*. After they have shown improvement according to the plan, they may even maintain the behaviors that they adopted as part of the plan. But because the plan was written to change behavior, it does not change the way that a teacher thinks.

	NOVICE	APPRENTICE	PRACTITIONER	MASTER TEACHER
Skill Development Goal	To acquire knowledge for, in, and of practice.	To apply principles to practice.	To assimilate skills and principles to develop seamless practice and adaptive expertise.	To adapt skills and principles to new, novel, or unpredictable situations and maintain mindful practice.
Evaluation Purpose	To clarify the difference between unsatisfactory and satisfactory performance.	To clarify the difference between satisfactory and effective performance.	To clarify the subtle difference between effective and excellent performance.	To provide objectivity and challenge to teaching practice.
Elaboration Method	Worked examples	Case studies	Action research	Problem-solving activities
Observation Approach	Walk-throughs	Walk-throughs and model lessons	Self-observation	Peer visits with reflection
Practice Type	Practice specific teaching behaviors	Practice one principle	Micropractice	Innovation
Feedback Type	Diagnostic	Prescriptive	Summary	Precise
Coaching Approach	Focus on specific skills	Focus on specific principles	Focus on synthesizing principles	Master classes and access to experts
Collaboration Approach	Learn from practitioners	Contribute to novices and learn from practitioners and master teachers	Mentor novices and practitioners, learn from master teachers	Articulate practice to novices, apprentices, and practitioners
Reflection Target	Reflect on the effect of concrete behaviors on student learning	Reflect on specific principles	Attend to their "teacher sense"	Articulate decision making

4
UNDERSTANDING AND IDENTIFYING WILL

Leadership should be born out of the understanding of the needs of those who would be affected by it.
—*Marian Anderson, The New York Times, July 22, 1951*

When I walked into Ms. Davis's classroom, I knew I was in trouble. Students were openly talking to their friends, fiddling with their cell phones, or sprawled across their desks asleep. No one was paying attention to Ms. Davis, who was droning away through PowerPoint slide after slide after boring slide. She didn't even notice me at first (her back was to the class while she read each bullet point on the screen), until a student got her attention.

"Oh, Dr. Jackson," she smiled, standing up from her seat. "We're just going over some notes." She asked her students to take out some paper to make sure that they were "getting these notes down," even as she assured them that all the slides would be posted to her class website by the end of the day. A few students, realizing that Ms. Davis was being observed, gamely complied; others rolled their eyes and continued their conversations or their naps.

Later, I reviewed my notes and tried to select two or three things to focus on in my report. So many things were wrong, I wasn't sure where to start. The next day, after giving Ms. Davis general feedback and sharing with her the data I collected, I moved to my recommendations.

"So, there are several things I think you need to work on for my next visit."

"OK. Sure." She smiled a little too brightly as she braced herself for my remarks.

Because many of her students were off task during her lecture, I first suggested we explore some ways to better engage them. Ms. Davis nodded along as I recommended that she work with the instructional coach on strategies for making her lectures more interactive. She might, perhaps, try using distributed review strategies or breaking periodically to give students a chance to summarize what they were learning. "And because your students seem very social," I added, "it may make sense to do a few paired summarizing activities, such as numbered heads, to give them a chance to interact with each other during the lecture."

"Great idea!" Ms. Davis smiled, nodded, and wrote it down.

This was going better than I had expected. I gave her a few more suggestions, shared some resources, discussed additional strategies, encouraged her to work with the instructional coach, handed her my write-up, and set up an informal observation for two weeks later.

When I arrived at her classroom for my follow-up observation, it was as if time had stood still. The kids were still disengaged, and Ms. Davis was plowing through another set of slides. When she noticed me, she clapped her hands and announced it was time for students to work with a partner. The students looked confused.

"What partner?" several of them asked.

"Just get a partner," Ms. Davis smiled. "Anyone will do. Come on, now. Does everyone have a partner?"

Slowly, reluctantly, the students paired up. Ms. Davis told them to summarize "the last two or three slides. Use your notes!" When the students protested that they hadn't taken notes—and some weren't even sure what "summarize" meant—she told them to "just use what you remember."

After 15 minutes of confused activity, Ms. Davis returned to her lecture. By that time, I had a full-on headache.

At our next meeting, I talked with Ms. Davis about how best to use distributed summarizing. I gave her an article that offered step-by-step instructions and encouraged her to observe another teacher in the school who used the strategy particularly well. Later, I spoke with the instructional coach, who agreed to help Ms. Davis plan lessons featuring distributed summarizing.

And yet: The next time I visited Ms. Davis's classroom, it was pretty much a repeat of the same scene.

I was at my wits' end. I had shared resources, modeled a strategy, explained it, and provided a tremendous amount of support. I'd suggested different options and strategies that might help. Despite all this, she was still lecturing the same way, and her instruction was as chaotic and ineffective as ever. She knew what she was "supposed" to do, but she wasn't doing it.

Ms. Davis didn't have a skill problem. She had a will problem.

What makes a teacher choose to help students each day? What makes some teachers support struggling learners or go above and beyond for a kid, whereas other teachers sit by and watch children fail? What makes one teacher choose to get better and another choose to stay stuck in mediocrity? What can you do to influence their choices?

Teacher will is what drives teachers to improve their craft and persist with students (or prevents them from doing so). It's what helps teachers embrace (or reject) new initiatives, try new strategies, work on their craft, and actively contribute to the school community. Teachers with high will work hard to grow professionally; they are more cooperative, engaged, and enthusiastic. Teachers with low will, however, become cynical and pessimistic; they resist change even when it is clearly what's best for students. They refuse to improve their craft even when offered the time and support to do so.

Sometimes low will manifests itself as direct opposition to a request or initiative, but other times low will is much more passive. Low-will teachers may agree to a change but then subtly undermine that change or ignore it altogether. To diagnose teacher will, you need to be able to identify the primary driver behind it. Once you understand an individual teacher's motivation, you can address it and in doing so support that teacher's path to mastery.

Distinguishing Between Low and High Will

Teacher skill is fairly obvious and easily measured; teacher will can be much less apparent and, thus, much more difficult to diagnose and address. Not only is will harder to detect than skill, it is also more variable and more likely to fluctuate throughout the school year. Many teachers start the year with a great deal of energy and enthusiasm, but circumstances (inside or outside of school) can erode their will over time. Other teachers may start the year with low will but, encountering the right kind of support, can increase their will over the course of the year. Although they are subtle, there are plenty of behavioral indicators of will that will help you distinguish low-will teachers from high-will teachers (see Figure 4.1).

Here are two suggestions to help your diagnosis.

Listen to what teachers say. Does the teacher complain about students and blame them for their lack of success, or does the teacher take responsibility and ownership of student success? Is the teacher cynical and pessimistic about teaching in general or optimistic, positive, and hopeful? Does the teacher criticize new initiatives and say "that will never work here," or does the teacher offer suggestions for how to make it work? Does the teacher get defensive in the face of feedback, or does the teacher engage in reflective conversations?

Watch what teachers do. Does the teacher's behavior reveal a commitment to students' mental, physical, and emotional welfare? Does the teacher seem willing to do whatever it takes to ensure that all students are successful? Does the teacher demonstrate high expectations for herself and her students? Is the teacher reflective about practice, and does she use feedback to improve her performance? Does the teacher actively participate in professional development and attempt to incorporate best practices in the classroom?

Figure 4.1   Common Will Indicators: Low and High

Low-Will Teachers . . .	High-Will Teachers . . .
Seem disinterested in improving their practice; are content with the way things are.	Constantly seek ways to learn, grow, and improve.
Are defensive about their practice.	Are reflective about their practice.
Grudgingly participate in professional development; may complain that they "knew this already."	Actively participate in professional development and look for ways to apply what they learn to their own practice.
Have trouble working on teams.	Make valuable contributions to teams.
Criticize new initiatives.	Suggest ways to improve new initiatives and make them work better.
Do only what is necessary or required.	Go above and beyond what is required.
Seem bored, lethargic, and disengaged.	Are active participants in their professional growth and development.
Resist feedback.	Seek feedback from colleagues and students and use feedback to improve.
Have low expectations for themselves and for students.	Maintain high expectations of themselves and their students.
Have trouble staying motivated.	Find ways to motivate themselves.
Give up easily.	Persevere with students and try to find ways to surmount challenges.
Allow students to fail with little or no intervention.	Proactively intervene with students and find ways to help even failing students be successful.
Can be inflexible regarding classroom rules, policies, deadlines, and procedures.	Adjust their practice to best meet the individual needs of each student.
Struggle to build personal relationships with colleagues, students, and parents.	Work to foster positive relationships with colleagues, students, and parents.
Hold ability-based beliefs about themselves and students.	Hold growth-oriented beliefs about themselves and students.
See students in terms of their deficits rather than their strengths.	Seek ways to help students capitalize on their strengths and overcome their learning challenges.

What Drives Teacher Will?

Although many leaders look for logical reasons to explain why a teacher is low will or high will, often a teacher's reasons for accepting or resisting change are illogical, based on something more primal. As Daniel H. Pink (2009) and many others have pointed out, to some extent, we are all driven by the desire for four basic feelings: autonomy, mastery, purpose, and belonging. Each of us, however, has a *primary will driver*—one of the four that matters more to us than the others and is key to our motivation.

It is difficult if not impossible for someone to stay motivated if his or her primary will driver is not met. For instance, teachers whose primary will driver is autonomy may be able to move forward with a new initiative even if they don't fully understand the purpose of what they are being asked to do; however, if their autonomy is threatened in some way—if they feel they are losing control over their own environment and destiny—they will shut down completely. Although it is important to understand that all teachers need autonomy, mastery, purpose, and belonging in order to thrive, to understand why a teacher is high or low will, you must identify that teacher's primary will driver. Let's take a closer look at all four of the possibilities.

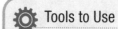 **Tools to Use**

For guidance in determining an individual teacher's primary will driver, see **Tool 2** in the Appendix.

Autonomy

Autonomy is the need to feel that you have some control over your activities and outcomes. Teachers who are motivated by autonomy need to feel self-directed, that they have some choice over what they do in the classroom and how they do it. A lack of autonomy significantly damages their will. Unfortunately, current trends in education can threaten teacher autonomy.

School systems throughout our country increasingly dictate what teachers should teach, and when and how they should teach it. Teachers who are required to be on page 57 of the curriculum guide by Tuesday feel that they cannot stop to spend time helping students acquire concepts. Districts and individual schools attempt to solve instructional challenges by embracing the latest educational research and best practices. They declare that "this year we will focus on rigor" or "for the next three years, we will develop better assessment practices." Although there is nothing wrong with these initiatives, teachers who need autonomy can feel that such initiatives dictate how they must teach.

In addition, as testing pressure continues to mount, many school leaders are encroaching more and more on teachers' planning time. In some schools, teachers' planning time is almost entirely co-opted by the school administration for team or group planning, test preparation, data analysis, and professional development. Teachers who need autonomy bristle at the erosion of their planning time and begin to resist fully participating in structured meetings and work sessions. Teachers who need autonomy also may struggle with working on assigned teams, feeling that this mandated collegiality where they must plan with their grade-alike or subject-alike partners is a waste of time. They would much rather work alone or with colleagues they choose.

Unfortunately, teachers who continually experience threats to or a lack of autonomy can develop learned helplessness, similar to students who repeatedly fail or receive negative feedback. These teachers have gotten to the point where they throw up their hands and ask, "Why bother?" Why bother thinking through their instructional practice and being reflective when they are only going to be told what to do anyway? Why bother trying to improve their instruction when the feedback they get is more directive than diagnostic—and often features the evaluator's pet instructional strategies rather than suggestions tailored to their own teaching style and needs? Why bother being a reflective practitioner when no one engages them in reflective conversations?

When teachers get to this point, they tend to do one of two things: If their skill is low, then they become passive, doing only what they are told and no more. If their skill is high, they often become rebellious and try to reassert their autonomy and sense of control through means that can be destructive to the school environment. They may try to fight new initiatives that threaten their autonomy or try to exert greater control over students as a way of trying to regain some of their autonomy.

Even high-will teachers can express a need for autonomy. If their skill is high, they may simply want to close their door and teach; any feedback from you feels like an intrusion. If their skill is low, they may seek help in terms of additional resources or strategies, but they will want to study these resources themselves and determine which of the strategies is the best fit for them.

You can recognize autonomy as the primary driver for teachers by listening to their complaints. Do they feel constrained by the curriculum or resent having to do things just like everyone else? Do they complain about their time being co-opted by structured activities in the school? Do they tend to resist any district or schoolwide mandates? If so, autonomy is probably a key driver.

Mastery

Teachers who are driven by a sense of mastery want to get better at something that matters, to master something new and engaging. They are curious. They love to experiment with their teaching, and they eagerly engage in professional development, often taking what they have learned and tweaking it until it becomes their own. Teachers who need mastery often get bored with the same routine year after year and seek new experiences and variety. They are always looking for something new to learn. If you want to kill the will of a mastery-driven teacher, force that teacher to teach the same thing the same way year after year. These teachers need novelty and challenge in order to stay motivated. Of the four will drivers, mastery is most related to a teacher's skill and most affected by it. High-skill teachers who also need mastery tend to be more motivated than low-skill teachers who need mastery.

Teachers driven by mastery seek feedback on their teaching practice. They want to know what you think about a new strategy they are trying and what suggestions you may have for improvement. They are interested in getting better, and any feedback that helps them do so—feedback that is focused on their individual practice, not pat and formulaic—is welcome. This includes feedback from students. They study their students to see what is working and what isn't working and adjust their practice accordingly. Mastery-driven teachers are more likely than other teachers to examine data and use data to tweak their practice.

Mastery-driven teachers are enthusiastic about professional development; they ask questions about how to apply what they are learning to their own practice and think about how what they are learning relates to their own teaching style and students' needs. They are usually the first to apply a new strategy or implement the latest district initiative. Avid early adopters, teachers driven by mastery typically figure out how to make a new strategy or initiative work and share what they are learning with their colleagues. They get excited about a new strategy or approach and want to present it at the next faculty meeting or share it with their team. They can get discouraged when their colleagues don't share their enthusiasm and may eventually prefer to work alone.

Unfortunately, teachers who need mastery tend to try to do everything and can get burned out. They get frustrated that they can't accomplish everything that they are asked to accomplish or that they aren't good at everything they expect to be good at. They tend to work really hard—staying late, devoting weekends to planning, attending summer workshops, participating in professional development after school, and reading professional articles and books. If their hard work pays off, they are even more motivated to learn as much as they can. But if their hard work doesn't yield results in terms of student achievement, their will can plummet.

High-will teachers express their need for mastery by seeking new professional development experiences, challenge, and novelty. They are constantly tweaking their practice, looking for ways to be more successful with students, and seeking feedback; their focus is on getting better. They can get frustrated if they are not successful with a particular student or group of students, but their frustration will lead them to try a different approach or seek additional advice from you or their colleagues.

Low-will teachers, however, typically express their need for mastery by giving up, and, although they may settle for mediocrity, they are not happy about it. They know what good teaching is, and they want to be good at teaching, but they have given up hope. Their frustration can quickly turn to pessimism; they begin to complain that the latest initiative can't be done or won't work. High-skill/low-will teachers who need mastery may even blame the students. Because they know pedagogy and have done everything they know to do to reach their students and it still hasn't worked, they assume that it must be the students' fault. They conclude that it's a hopeless case and make excuses for why "those kids" cannot meet standards.

You can usually tell if teachers are driven by mastery by looking at how they approach their craft. Do they work hard to get better at teaching? Do they get frustrated if they do not meet the goals they have set for themselves? Do they spend most of their time and energy trying to make something work? If so, it is likely that they are driven by mastery.

Purpose

Many teachers are attracted to the profession because of a clear sense of purpose. They want to change lives. They want to open doors for children. They want to save the world. What gets them up in the morning is a higher calling, a cause greater than themselves. This is a natural human tendency. On some level, we all need a sense of purpose to motivate us. But teachers whose primary driver is purpose cannot work well without it. They need to see the big picture—and be part of it—in order to function.

Teachers who are motivated by purpose need to know why they are doing what they are doing; they will question the reason behind an initiative or suggestion and will not move until they have an answer. Their questions may sometimes seem like stalling tactics, but they are not. If you cannot help them answer the "why?" then it will be hard to keep them focused. Once they understand the why, they are ready to move forward.

Teachers who need purpose also tend to focus on the vision and mission of the organization. If they cannot understand or embrace the vision, they have difficulty staying motivated. They need to be able to see how they fit in the overall vision and mission of the organization, and to understand their role in the greater vision of the school or district. They want to be part of conversations that help them consider the connections between their beliefs and actions; the social, historical, political, economic, and cultural contexts of schooling; and their students' lives. They need time and opportunity to examine their own personal and professional values, beliefs, theories, and assumptions and how these relate to the organizational and social contexts of teaching and learning.

Purpose-driven teachers will get discouraged if their vision conflicts with their duties, responsibilities, or role in the school. If they cannot understand the thinking behind the curriculum, they will have a hard time implementing it with fidelity; if a district initiative conflicts with their own values and personal mission, they experience real cognitive dissonance.

These teachers love to engage in philosophical conversations about the purpose of education and what it means to be effective in the classroom. They are motivated by big-picture conversations about the higher calling of education and get impatient with discussing details. "Why teach?" is more important than what or how to do it.

Low-will teachers who are driven by purpose tend to express cynicism about education and the direction of the profession. This cynicism can manifest itself in a couple of ways: They can be openly hostile against a new idea or initiative (based on principle), or they can be passively resistant, giving lip service to an idea but secretly doing what aligns to their vision. Low-will teachers driven by purpose also suffer from low expectations. They have given up on believing that they can ever accomplish the high ideals they hold and have lowered their expectations to what they feel is reasonable. Because they still hold onto their ideals, they are never fully comfortable with their lowered expectations and can become really disillusioned and bitter. Many eventually leave the profession.

High-will teachers driven by purpose tend to be idealistic. They are on a mission, and their ideals drive them to hone their craft so that they can better serve the greater good. They want to inspire children, and they have high expectations for their students. It is tough for these teachers to balance their lofty goals for students with the harsh realities many face. If they are not careful, their idealism can be shattered when it brushes up against the brutal facts of their situation.

You can usually recognize teachers driven by purpose by their questions. Do they ask the hard questions, typically prefaced by some form of "why"? Do they want to engage in philosophical conversations rather than deal with the more practical demands of their jobs? If so, it is likely that they are driven by purpose.

Belonging

Teachers who need belonging need to feel they are a part of the team. If they feel that you like them and respect their work, they will work doubly hard to support you, even if they don't support the particular change or initiative you are trying to institute. They value relationships, and if the relationships are not right, they find it hard to generate the motivation they need to be master teachers. They spend time tending relationships by seeking connection, resolving conflict, and building rapport. It's not that they won't spend time on other aspects of their jobs, but they will focus on building relationships first, even if it is at the sacrifice of more pressing duties.

For teachers who are motivated by belonging, it isn't just the collegial relationships that matter; it's also the relationships they have with their students. They will work very hard to cultivate positive relationships with students, sometimes at the sacrifice of moving through the curriculum or holding students to high standards. If their students resist these relationships, these teachers have a hard time helping them learn.

If belonging is a teacher's primary will driver, that teacher's ability to be effective in the classroom is almost entirely driven by the quality of his or her relationships with others. I have seen high-will teachers quickly become low will when forced to work alone or to work with people they did not like. I've seen low-will teachers become high will when they felt included, liked, and respected. The same is true with teachers' relationships with students. I have seen high-will teachers give up on students when they could not forge a connection and low-will teachers persist with students they liked. If the relationships are in place and these teachers feel that they belong, they are very effective instructors. If there is a broken relationship somewhere, they struggle to function well.

Paradoxically, teachers for whom belonging is the primary driver may also express their need for belonging by almost antisocial behavior. Often, the teachers who are the hardest to like or get along with are the ones who need belonging the most. They want to be liked, but because they don't know how to get others to like them, they engage in behaviors that drive others away.

Low-will teachers may express their need for belonging by hanging out in the staff lounge with their colleagues during their planning period or complaining about you or a particular initiative to their colleagues during lunchtime. They may try to turn other teachers against you or form informal groups to actively or passively resist your changes. If their skill is high, they may go out of their way to show everyone how good they are and resist your efforts to give them feedback to the contrary. Often, low-will teachers driven by belonging insist that they are already master teachers and refuse to accept feedback, suggestions, or recommendations.

They want to be seen as effective and may hide their teaching challenges so that they can look good in your eyes and in the eyes of their colleagues. They may also struggle with forging positive relationships with students, attempting to be their students' friends. If they feel that their students do not like them, they may unintentionally do things that antagonize the students, almost as punishment for not being accepted.

High-will teachers can express their need for belonging by seeking a relationship with you and their colleagues. They may drop by your office just to talk about their day or to seek your input on something they are working on. The content of the conversation isn't as important to them as the connection they feel with you. High-will teachers driven by belonging also work hard at connecting with students. They usually are the ones that even the most difficult students trust and seek out. When successful, they can motivate students to do things they might not ordinarily do—often students will do things for these teachers that they won't do for anyone else.

The easiest way to spot teachers who need belonging is by looking at how they approach relationships with students and their peers. Is their primary question always "Who?"? Do they typically do whatever you ask of them, even if they disagree? Or, if you don't have a relationship with them, do they resist your efforts to lead them regardless of whether they accept the logic of your argument, the soundness of your initiative, or the urgency of the mandate before them? If so, it is likely that they are driven by belonging.

Back to Ms. Davis

Once I understood that Ms. Davis had a will problem and not a skill problem, I changed my tack. Instead of plying her with new resources, feedback, and additional strategies (and trying to hold her accountable for implementing them), I decided to stop by her classroom one day for a chat.

"I've done you a disservice," I started.

"What do you mean?" she asked, bracing herself for my next onslaught of strategies.

"I've spent the last month trying to push you to implement strategies you really don't want to implement," I explained.

Ms. Davis tried to protest. "No, no, I've tried to do things like you asked."

I shook my head. "Not really. You don't want to teach that way."

She was silent. Waiting.

"I am giving you strategies you really don't want to use," I continued. "Why didn't you just tell me that?"

Ms. Davis was quiet for a moment. Finally, she whispered, "I thought I didn't have a choice."

"I'm sorry you felt that way," I said. We were both silent for a moment. Then I continued. "The thing is, the way that you are teaching isn't working."

"But that's my teaching style," Ms. Davis protested. "You want me to become one of those Stepford teachers and teach like everyone else. I've been teaching for more than 20 years, and I have my own way of doing things. All these fads, they come and go. I've found something that works for me, and that's what I intend to do. You keep trying to change me and make me teach like you."

A light went on: *She needed autonomy.*

I had been so focused on trying to change Ms. Davis's teaching that I hadn't helped her understand why her teaching needed changing in the first place.

What I did next was show her data from my last few observations regarding how her students were responding to her instruction, focusing my feedback on the effect her teaching style was having on students. Once I stopped trying to tell Ms. Davis how to teach, she relaxed and admitted that her instruction probably could use some improvement. But instead of telling her how to improve, I worked on helping her to commit to improve. Once I had her commitment, I could shift to helping her choose how to improve and to providing her with resources, feedback, support, and accountability.

I started to see a change in Ms. Davis. She didn't magically transform into a master teacher, but she did start making progress in that direction. She was much more open to my feedback, came up with strategies she would attempt on her own, and was more attuned to the effect her teaching had on her students.

I tell this story because it underscores how important it is to get the diagnosis right. Once you understand that you are facing a will problem and you understand its basis, you can determine the best leadership course of action. The better you understand what is driving teacher behavior, the better you will be able to select a leadership approach that will actually move teachers forward rather than waste time and resources by jumping in with a solution that is not likely to work.

YES, BUT . . .
Some of my teachers just seem impossible to figure out. What if I can't identify the root reason for a teacher's resistance?

It is easy to diagnose the primary will driver when people seek help and advice or directly resist change, but often people can *seem* to support change and then passively resist moving forward. These "passive resisters" make it very difficult to determine the underlying reason for their low will.

Many leaders confront passive resistance by confidently charging forward, assuming that they have the support and cooperation of the passive resisters, only to discover too late that not everyone was fully on board. Later, when the initiative fails, they think it was because there was some flaw in the initiative itself rather than understanding that the initiative was undermined by passive resistance.

To diagnose core will issues in the face of passive resistance, pay attention to the "logical" reasons people present for not making the change. If they are asking for more data, their primary will driver is probably purpose, and they are looking for a justification for making the change. If they argue that there isn't enough time, their primary will driver may be autonomy, and they are concerned that the change may further limit their ability to plan their own days. If they suggest that you build the capacity of the team first, their primary driver may be mastery, and they are worried that they won't be able to implement the change effectively. If they want to get buy-in from everyone first before moving forward, their will driver may be belonging. Rather than trying to overcome their logical reasons for resistance by offering logical arguments of your own, listen to their reasons and look for the underlying need those reasons imply.

CHAPTER 4 TAKEAWAYS
Identifying the Primary Will Driver

IF TEACHERS...	THEY NEED...
• Complain that they are no longer able to be creative as a teacher • Resist structure • Want to do things their own way • Passively or aggressively resist new initiatives that prescribe how to teach • Find ways to exert control over their environment • Thrive best when left alone • Are good at figuring out how to make things work for them and their students • Have their own unique teaching style and strategies • Complain that they no longer have any free time to plan as they please • Resent that they have to follow a prescribed curriculum and pacing guide • Prefer to simply "close their door and teach" • Often come up with innovative ways of teaching • Do not take suggestions or recommendations well and resist prescriptive feedback	Autonomy
• Seek novelty and challenge • Constantly tweak their practice • Seek feedback and act on it • Try new techniques, strategies, and resources • Ask for support to attend conferences, workshops, or online courses • Get frustrated when something isn't working the way they'd hoped • Ask for permission to try something new or seek funding for some innovative idea • Complain that something is not innovative • Become enamored with the latest technology or technique and attempt to incorporate it in their classrooms • Resist doing things the same way year after year after year • Complain of being bored	Mastery

Identifying the Primary Will Driver *continued*

IF TEACHERS...	THEY NEED...
• Need to understand and embrace the vision and mission in order to be motivated • Need to understand the reason behind an initiative before moving forward • Talk about what's best for children • Have lofty ideals • Have very high expectations for students • Seek to inspire students and to be inspired • Justify what they are doing by connecting it to a higher purpose • Get frustrated by discussions of minutia and prefer big-picture conversations • Have clear reasons for why they do what they do	Purpose
• Focus on forging relationships • Seek approval from the school administration or colleagues • Forge relationships with students before focusing on teaching • Work well on teams • Need social interaction • Share what they are doing in the classroom and additional resources with others • Seek feedback, interaction, and engagement • Are able to reach the most difficult students and earn their trust • Tend to justify instructional decisions based on "who" rather than "what" or "why" • May themselves be socially awkward	Belonging

5
ADDRESSING WILL

What you have to do and the way you have to do it is incredibly simple. Whether you are willing to do it, that's another matter.

—*Peter F. Drucker*

Ms. McKay wasn't a bad teacher. In fact, she could be very effective in the classroom, and, depending on the day you stopped by, she was sometimes quite good. She worked hard at planning rigorous instructional experiences for her 7th grade students, was an engaging lecturer, and over the previous two years had managed to raise her students' test scores. And yet her principal, Mr. Williams, wanted her gone.

"*She's* your worst teacher?" I asked incredulously after doing a walk-through with Mr. Williams.

"She's a nightmare," he moaned, rubbing his temples. "She won't accept feedback on her teaching, she thinks she knows everything, she's horrible on teams, and nobody wants to work with her."

When I countered that Ms. McKay's practice was instructionally sound, Mr. Williams insisted that didn't matter. "I would rather have a poor teacher who is willing to learn than a decent one who completely wrecks my culture," he declared.

I understood this principal's dilemma. What he had on his hands was a classic low-will/high-skill teacher, in many ways the most frustrating type and also the most difficult to move—not just toward mastery but also "out the door."

"You'll never get rid of her, you know," I warned Mr. Williams. "And I don't know that you should. She's a good teacher! With a little help, she could be a master teacher."

Mr. Williams looked at me for a moment and then reached for the phone and dialed the number of the school's instructional coach. "Andrea, would you come in here for a second?"

A minute later, Andrea had joined us. Mr. Williams shut the office door, gestured for her to sit, and then invited her to tell me about all the ways they had tried to help Ms. McKay become—and here he used air quotes—"a master teacher."

Andrea rolled her eyes. "Ughhh. We have tried everything." She began to tick off the list on her fingers. "We have coached her, we've changed her team three times, we moved her to a new grade level, we've given her warnings, we've tried talking to her—and she just argues with us," Andrea said, clearly exasperated. "We have observed her class and given her feedback, which she ignores; we've sent her to workshops over the summer and during the school year. And nothing's worked."

"Are you sure that nothing's worked?" I asked. "All that, and you haven't seen even a small improvement in her instruction?"

Andrea thought for a moment. "I mean, sure, I see some improvement in her instruction. But her instruction's never really been the problem. Ms. McKay isn't a bad teacher, but she won't listen to us, and she argues with us all the time. She's a pain to work with."

Mr. Williams chimed in, "I met with her last year and told her that I thought she should look for a job elsewhere."

"Wow." I was a little surprised at his frankness. "What was her reaction?"

"She cried, and then she went right on back to being the same way she was. And she's still here." He shook his head.

"I don't want you to think that we are bullies," Andrea added. "I was there during that conversation, and Mr. Williams simply told her that he didn't think that she was happy here and maybe she should consider finding a place where she could be happy. He offered to help her."

"So let me see if I understand," I said. "You've tried to help her by giving her better training, giving her better feedback, and changing her team and grade level."

They both nodded.

"Well, it seems to me that those things are all designed to improve her skill, but skill isn't her problem. *Will* is."

"Yes, she's unwilling to learn," Mr. Williams declared. "And if somebody is unwilling to learn, then they don't belong in this building."

"Do you think you can change her will?" I asked.

"You can't change somebody's will," Mr. Williams replied, firmly. "Either they want to get better or they don't."

"I've tried talking to her," Andrea chimed in. "She won't listen. How can you help somebody who won't listen?"

This is a situation I've seen many times: instructional leaders frustrated by a low-will teacher and convinced that will is something intractable, that they can't make people want to do something they don't want to do. But people change their will all the time, eagerly buying into something that they initially resisted or resisting something they first supported.

The problem is that you cannot solve a will problem with a skill solution. If you want to change teachers' will, you can't do it by sending them to more workshops, providing more feedback, or offering more coaching—these are all skill solutions. If you want to change teachers' will, you need will solutions, and in many ways these are a lot harder to implement. They are not cut and dried. They require a relationship. They require you to really understand your teachers' motivations.

If you want to motivate the teachers you serve to get better, if you want to serve your students better, and if you want to do something important and positive, you need to understand how to move teacher will. To do that, you need to understand why they might resist change.

Reasons for Resistance

Let's look at the five main reasons teachers' will tends to wane, using a framework articulated by Karla Reiss (2006).

Limiting Beliefs

The term *limiting beliefs* describes a set of views and theories that teachers may have acquired from their own experience as learners, from feedback they've received from teachers or their own parents, or from misinterpreting feedback they receive from students and their educational colleagues. They are the inner critic that prevents them from achieving mastery in teaching and curbs their professional growth. Limiting beliefs may include "I will never get these kids to pass the test by March," "I am not good with working with special needs students," or "I'll never be as good as Mr. So-and-So."

Assumptions

Assumptions are the result of taking a past experience and believing that any similar future experience will have the exact same result. Assumptions feed resistance by keeping teachers from trying new things or being open to new experiences. Some examples you may be familiar with include "I'll never reach that student; I've been unsuccessful with his type before," "We tried that before, and it was excruciating," and "These workshops are all the same."

Fear

Fear is perhaps the biggest and most debilitating reason for resistance. You see it when teachers don't want to try something new or step outside an established comfort zone because doing so makes them feel threatened in some way. Sometimes what we are asking them to do threatens their sense of who they are as teachers. Other times, what we are asking them to do threatens their sense of security and poses a new, frightening unknown. Either way, fear incites an intense fight, flight, or freeze response: "There is no way I am doing that. I'm calling the union!" or "I guess I need to look for another job at another school," or even complete silence and inaction.

Judgments

When teachers form a negative opinion about an idea or initiative, or about the person sponsoring the new idea or initiative, and that opinion keeps them from acting, they have lapsed into judgment. Judgments can influence whether teachers interpret a person, idea, initiative, or feedback positively or negatively and get in the way of willingness to take action. When teachers judge, it may sound like this: "That kid is lazy," "My principal is only doing this so that he can get a promotion," "My team leader doesn't like me, so she is always picking on my teaching," or "This is the superintendent's pet project, and *that's* why they are pushing it."

Obstacles

An obstacle is any external factor that seems to stand in the way of or prevent us from reaching a goal or doing what we want. Rather than focus on how to overcome an obstacle, teachers may focus on the obstacle itself, conclude there is no way around it, and give up. Teachers who resist because of an obstacle say things like "I don't know how I am supposed to teach when they cut the funding to my program in half" or "These students face so many challenges before they even walk in the door. How am I supposed to overcome those challenges and get them focused on learning?" or "This new teacher evaluation system is forcing me to teach to the test in order to get a good evaluation."

All these reasons for resistance play out differently for each of the four will drivers we've discussed. Finding an individual's primary motivator— autonomy, mastery, purpose, or belonging—is the key to breaking through these barriers to change, building teacher will, and getting that individual on—or back on—the path to masterful teaching.

Building Will in Autonomy-Driven Teachers

Teachers who need autonomy want to have some choice in what and how they teach. Even if you cannot give teachers complete freedom in these areas, it is important to recognize and honor teachers' autonomy needs in order to keep them motivated. This means that you must, to the extent possible, allow these teachers to define when, where, and how best to get their work done, holding them accountable for the results. The more choice you provide for these teachers, the more motivated they will become.

Limiting a teacher's autonomy is one of the main ways that we destroy teacher will, and yet many leadership books and coaching manuals actually encourage us to do just that. They tell us that it is our job, as instructional leaders, to prescribe better teaching strategies and techniques. They tell us that we should always be prepared to offer teachers a better solution to their teaching challenges. Such advice does more than just lead us to infringe on teachers' autonomy; when we get in the habit of telling teachers how to teach, we rob them of the chance to think through their teaching challenges for themselves. We do their thinking for them.

In many schools, we hold teachers accountable for initiatives they had no part in creating. It's rather like being asked to cook a meal you didn't plan, with groceries you didn't buy, using recipes you didn't create, in a kitchen you didn't equip, under time constraints you didn't set. Oh—and you'll be fired if the food isn't absolutely delicious. This might make a great "reality" show, but in actual reality, it's no wonder so many teachers' wills are sapped. Why should they continue to work to get better if we are only going to prescribe to them what they should do and when and how they should do it? Helping teachers who need autonomy must always leave them with a sense of control.

There is a huge difference, however, between autonomy and anarchy. Many instructional leaders try to avoid the appearance of being too controlling by handing all of the control over to teachers. They try to appease teachers by giving them complete autonomy, allowing them to do whatever they want as long as the kids learn. This isn't leadership; it's an abdication of responsibility. It is important to find the right mix of autonomy and freedom, choice and conformity.

One of the best ways to find this middle ground is to balance autonomy with accountability, and control with responsibility. Involve teachers in setting the vision, establishing the parameters within which they must work, and identifying the outcomes they must hit. Then invite teachers to take the lead on determining the best way to get there. Engage them in every stage of the process, but hold them accountable for specific outcomes. Don't micromanage them; you must allow them some freedom to decide how they will meet the goals that you have established together. Giving teachers more responsibility and accountability also gives them a greater sense of control over their outcomes. In fact, the more autonomy you give, the more accountability you can require.

I first learned this lesson when working with Mr. Flay, who was one of the best math teachers at my school. Not only did he really understand math, he also knew how to help his *students* really understand it. Mr. Flay—Peter—was also a hard worker, staying late most days to design lessons, work with students, and grow professionally. He loved his job, and what he wanted most was to be left alone to do that job. Because he was such an effective teacher, that's exactly what we did most of the time: We allowed Peter to close his door and teach.

Unfortunately for Peter, our district adopted mandatory co-planning and participation in professional learning communities, both of which would require Peter to meet with his subject-alike and grade-alike colleagues to co-plan and collaborate. After the first mandatory co-planning meeting, Peter stormed into my office, calling the meeting "a ridiculous waste of time." He had better things to do than to sit in a room and write lessons he'd already written; he also didn't want to be "forced to do something their way when my way works for me." Peter didn't see any value in the co-planning process, believing it led to implementing "cookie-cutter lesson plans" that eliminated valuable individual approaches.

I explained that this process was a district mandate; we needed to give it some time. And I decided to attend the next co-planning meeting to see for myself what was going on and try to figure out how to make the process work for Peter.

The meeting was an eye-opener. As it turned out, I didn't just have one teacher who needed autonomy, I had an entire team of them! None of the teachers was actually co-planning. What they were doing instead was bringing their own plans to the meeting and trying to get everyone else to adopt these as the grade-level standard. Given all the autonomy-driven teachers I had, Peter was right: It really *was* a waste of time.

How could I fix this? The purpose of the co-planning mandate was to get teachers to collaborate in order to learn from each other, achieve grade-level consistency, and create a culture of collegiality. But these were teachers who were used to doing their own thing. How could I get these teachers, who all required a high level of autonomy, to work together?

My solution was to build some flexibility into how they collaborated. Rather than focus on individual lesson plans, I thought maybe the team should focus on more global concerns affecting their grade level and subject. At their next meeting, I proposed that they spend their collaborative planning time determining what were the "need to knows" and the "nice to knows" of the curriculum. I assigned the math coach to facilitate the meetings and tasked the team with identifying the most important skills students needed coming into each grade and the most critical skills students needed to learn in order to have mastered the curriculum for that grade level. I asked them to create common assessments that reflected these priorities and to agree to administer them four times each quarter. Other than that, I explained, they each had autonomy in their classrooms; they could teach the content however they thought best.

At the end of two months, the team had identified the essential skills and had designed a few common assessments. We managed to strike a good balance between autonomy and accountability, and the teachers were much happier with using their team time this way rather than planning individual lessons. Student achievement also increased significantly in math for that grade level as a result of the clarity and focus generated by thinking through the need-to-knows.

Although this story had a happy ending, it wasn't easy getting there. It can be challenging to determine where to allow teachers latitude and what areas are nonnegotiable. Remember that your goal for moving autonomous teachers is to help them balance their need for the freedom to develop their own personal style of teaching with the responsibility to improve student outcomes.

In addition to addressing teachers' sources of resistance (see Figure 5.1), you can support their need for autonomy by allowing them leeway in "the 5 T's": *time, team, task, technique,* and *territory.*

Time

One of the most common complaints I hear from teachers is that they never have enough time to implement all the initiatives that they've been assigned. Autonomy-driven teachers, particularly low-will ones, resent having their time co-opted by prescribed team planning or other structured activities; they would rather spend the time doing things that make the most sense to *them*, that support *their* practice, and that *their* students

Figure 5.1   Responding to Autonomy-Driven Teachers'
                     Sources of Resistance

Source	Message	Response
Limiting beliefs	"I don't like working with others."	Help teachers to focus on what they can accomplish through working with others. Balance the need for teams with teachers' need to work on their own; limit conformity requirements or offer some options for teachers to customize what they develop as a result of group planning.
Assumptions	"This new strategy, initiative, or process will limit me in some way."	Give teachers resources and allow them time to digest them. Then engage them in a conversation about the strategy or initiative and how they might apply it to their own practice.
Fear	"I am afraid to lose control."	Offer teachers more than one suggestion or strategy, and then allow them to choose among your suggestions. When you can, offer suggestions and recommendations rather than directives.
Judgments	"They just want to control me."	Use noncontrolling language. Rather than "you must" or "we should," shift to language that implies some form of choice such as "have you considered" or "think about."
Obstacles	"This new person, idea, or initiative is limiting my freedom of choice."	Shift teachers' focus away from the limitations of the new person, idea, or initiative and toward their options. Show teachers the choices they have within the constraints of the new initiative.

need. Give teachers some control over how they spend their time by building unstructured time into their day or week.

Team

Although it is important that teachers collaborate as grade-alike and subject-alike colleagues, give teachers some flexibility, and let them choose their own team when they work on more personal goals. For example, allow teachers to choose which colleagues they will engage in peer observation and feedback, or let teachers pick colleagues to collaborate with on certain professional development goals.

Task

Attending to task autonomy means stepping back and allowing teachers freedom in how they accomplish their various responsibilities. For example, try offering them choices about which schoolwide goals they will work on and then establishing committees around each goal. Or step back and offer them choices about how they approach the (required) curriculum, which activities they teach, and which texts they use. Although you may not want to or be able to give teachers complete autonomy over what they do each day, you can give them some say about their main responsibilities or what they are required to do during a given week.

Technique

One of the biggest mistakes to make with teachers whose primary driver is autonomy is to go into their classrooms and tell them how to teach. Any time we prescribe to them a particular teaching strategy, we risk completely destroying their will.

Instead of telling these teachers *how* to teach, point out the area of their instructional practice that needs improving, explain to them the effect of their current teaching technique on students, and then allow them to determine the best way to address the problem. Give low-skill teachers a choice between two alternatives you select. Let high-skill teachers choose their own strategies and think through their instructional challenges. You can support their decision making through facilitative or coaching conversations and can even suggest specific techniques should they ask for them, but allow them to come to their own conclusions about how they will teach differently or better themselves.

Territory

Allow teachers a lot of leeway when it comes to how they arrange their classroom space. I had a colleague who occasionally pushed all of the desks against the wall and conducted classroom discussions with students sprawled on the floor or lounging in beanbag chairs. It rattled my traditional sensibilities, but she believed that her students were much more willing to participate in class discussion that way. I never tested her theory, but I do know that giving her the latitude to arrange her classroom in a way that she felt best met her students' needs allowed her the freedom to reach students in a way that worked best for both her teaching style and her class's learning preferences.

Checkpoint Summary

*Build the will of **autonomy-driven** teachers by giving them choices in the 5 T's: time, team, task, technique, and territory.*

TOOLS FOR WILL DEVELOPMENT	RESULTING IN
Time considerations	A greater sense of control and focus
Team considerations	An increased willingness to work collaboratively
Task considerations	More productivity, engagement, and creativity
Technique considerations	More buy-in to district mandates and a greater sense of ownership
Territory considerations	A feeling of independence and individuality that may combat a sense of too many demands for conformity

Building Will in Mastery-Driven Teachers

Mastery-driven teachers need to believe that their abilities are matched to the challenges they face. To stay motivated, they need to believe that they can be successful at their jobs (however they define success). When these teachers are not successful, they can get frustrated and become cynical—not only about their own practice but also about the teaching profession as a whole.

Mrs. Harris was a perfect example of a teacher who needed mastery. When I first met Lindsey, it was a joy to visit her classroom. She was creative and engaging and utilized the very best practices for her students, who thrived in her social studies classroom. I would often stop in at Lindsey's classroom at the end of a stressful day to remind myself what good teaching looked like. She was simply one of the very best teachers in the school . . . until our district adopted a new curriculum.

Lindsey spent the summer studying the new curriculum, and what she found was dismaying. She disagreed with many of the choices the curriculum writers had made, felt that the essential questions were too pat, and believed that the curriculum cheated students of some key concepts that were vital to her subject. In order to implement the curriculum, she believed she'd have to swap many of her best lesson plans and activities for book work and lectures, both of which were antithetical to her interactive teaching style.

Lindsey started to feel that the new curriculum was making her a bad teacher. On my next visit to her classroom, I was surprised by her lifeless delivery and the dryness of her instruction. Concerned, I stopped in again after school.

"Do you see what I'm talking about?" Lindsey asked as soon as I had walked through the door.

"What do you mean?" I asked, startled by the vehemence of her question.

"That new curriculum. It's awful!" She moaned. "It's turning me into the kind of teacher I hate: nothing but lecture and book work and testing. Rinse and repeat. I'm going crazy."

"But Lindsey, you're a fabulous teacher," I said. "Surely you can make it work. Can you find a way to combine units to give yourself more time for the interactive, hands-on learning you like to do?"

"Robyn, I've tried that!" Lindsey said. "I've tried everything. But in order to cover all the content they want me to cover, I've got to drag kids through the curriculum. There is no time for interactivity. I can't teach this way."

Although I thought Lindsey's frustration would dissipate and that she would figure things out, I was wrong. Lindsey only got worse. She became very cynical, complaining about the school district, getting sarcastic about the profession, and even, incredibly, starting to blame the students. I called her into my office for a talk.

"Lindsey, what's going on? This isn't like you," I began.

She hung her head and sighed. "I know," she admitted. "I know." And then she started to cry.

I handed her a tissue and waited. She began to tell me how frustrated she was and how she felt like she was becoming a bad teacher. She couldn't make the new curriculum work no matter what she tried, and she was convinced that she was cheating her students of a valuable learning experience.

"I am thinking that maybe I need to leave teaching," she announced.

Facing the prospect of losing one of my most talented teachers, I panicked a little, and then I got to work. I knew that Lindsey needed mastery in order to be motivated; she felt that our new curriculum prevented her from achieving mastery. I realized that switching grade levels wouldn't solve the problem; the entire curriculum at each grade level was being revamped, and she would simply face the same frustration. Then I remembered that she was double-certified in social studies and in ESL. At the time, I was completing the master schedule for the following year and needed a new ESL teacher. When I suggested the switch to her, Lindsey got a faraway look in her eyes. She was already figuring out how to make it work.

By the next semester, Lindsey was a different person: thriving with her new students and her new subject area, spending her personal time learning more and more about her craft. I had paired her with a veteran ESL teacher, and the two of them got along so well that they spent hours planning together and coming up with creative ways to reach their students. Lindsey was finally doing something at which she felt she could be successful. She loved the challenge her new position provided and was excited about teaching again. She loved the novelty of her new subject and was energized by learning new strategies and pushing her own teaching to the next level. As a result, she found ways to reach her new students that were, quite frankly, amazing.

That's the thing about teachers driven by mastery. They are often the best teachers in the building, and they thrive when they feel that their abilities are a match for the challenges they face. But they can become very frustrated when what they are doing isn't working and they don't know how to improve. Over time, their lack of mastery and of the right kind of support can devastate their will. The good news is that if you can keep them interested, challenged, and feeling successful, they will thrive in the classroom, and their students will thrive as well.

In addition to addressing mastery-driven teachers' sources of resistance (see Figure 5.2), you can provide them with specific types of support: deliberate practice, frequent growth-oriented feedback, challenge, and novelty.

Figure 5.2　　Responding to Mastery-Driven Teachers'
　　　　　　　　Sources of Resistance

Source	Message	Response
Limiting beliefs	"I'll never get good at this."	Shape your suggestions, recommendations, and requests in terms of what teachers can accomplish. Focus on how following your request can help them achieve a particular goal. Provide growth-oriented feedback that shows them how they are progressing toward their goal and reinforce the idea that any teacher can get better with the right kind of practice.
Assumptions	"This new strategy will fail just like the last one did."	Point out the differences between what you are asking them to do and what they did before; give them the steps involved in trying the new strategy. Provide frequent feedback throughout the process to keep them focused on the present, not the past.
Fear	"I am afraid to fail."	Lessen the threat of failure by setting smaller goals rather than one big goal. Provide growth-oriented rather than evaluative feedback.
Judgments	"That is too hard." "Other people think I am not good at my job."	Break the process into smaller steps to help teachers experience incremental successes. Praise teachers' efforts rather than their abilities.
Obstacles	"This new person, idea, or initiative is keeping me from being good at my job."	Set up the obstacle as a challenge to overcome and help teachers work toward overcoming that challenge. Provide resources and flexibility to adjust the new initiative to better fit their teaching style while still honoring the initiative's goals or requirements.

Deliberate Practice

Deliberate practice is designed to improve a specific aspect of a teacher's performance. First, set clear objectives. What is it that they want to master? Next, identify specific things they will do to grow their practice. Perhaps they will try a new teaching technique or implement a new grading system; maybe they will alter their questioning strategies or attempt a new way of planning. Help them identify specific steps they will take to improve their teaching. Give them time to practice and reflect on their practice. They can collect data to see how effective their practice has been. Finally, use feedback to help them adjust their practice to better improve their performance, and continue to track their results. Deliberate practice can help teachers see dramatic improvement in their performance, increase their confidence, and boost their mastery of teaching.

Frequent Growth-Oriented Feedback

Teachers who seek mastery need frequent feedback to help them assess their progress. Feedback should be immediate, nonevaluative, and focused on helping them grow. Tell them what they are doing right, identify what is still not working, and give them suggestions for improvement. You don't have to be the only one to provide feedback; mastery-driven teachers can learn from peer observations with feedback, data from students, or classroom "red flags" that will alert teachers that they are headed in the wrong direction. (For instance, if a teacher is working on framing the learning better, a "red flag" might be that students cannot articulate the day's objective midway through the class period.) Feedback gives teachers tangible affirmation of what is working and a clear indication of what is not working. It shows mastery-driven teachers exactly how they need to adjust in order to reach mastery.

Challenge

Teachers who seek mastery need new challenges in order to stay motivated. If they feel that their skills are too far above the tasks that they are given, they get bored. You can fuel the motivation of these teachers by asking them to try a new teaching method or refine a particular teaching skill. Invite them to attempt a new certification area or go for a teaching award. Give them a schoolwide problem to tackle, and ask them to share solutions with their colleagues. Introduce new challenges to their day-to-day responsibilities, ensuring that the challenge isn't too far beyond their abilities and skills.

Novelty

Although some teachers are content to teach the same thing the same way year after year, teachers who are motivated by mastery need novelty from time to time. Give them new challenges to keep them engaged. Change their teaching responsibilities or put them on a new team. Ask them to teach a different subject or work with a different group of students.

📝 Checkpoint Summary

*Build the will of **mastery-driven** teachers by helping them see the way forward and navigate the path.*

TOOLS FOR WILL DEVELOPMENT	RESULTING IN
Deliberate practice	More effective instruction and improved confidence
Frequent growth-oriented feedback	Increased motivation, insight into what is and is not working, and clarity on how to move forward
Appropriate challenge	Increased engagement, renewed energy and focus, and (often) new ideas/contributions for the overall instructional program
Novelty	Decreased boredom

Building Will in Purpose-Driven Teachers

Purpose-driven teachers need to feel that they can incorporate their deeply held values into their day-to-day work. They will bring energy, focus, commitment, and perseverance to their jobs if they feel that their work truly matters. However, if they start to feel that their work has no real purpose, they will become unmotivated.

Teachers who need purpose can struggle to align their practice with their educational values. They need help seeing the connection between the rationale and underlying core values of what you are asking them to do and their own values or ideals. Without this understanding, it is hard for them to remain motivated. If you are unclear about the purpose of the work you are asking teachers to perform or have trouble identifying and articulating the vision and mission, your purpose-driven teachers will have trouble maintaining high will.

Sometimes this quest for purpose can look a lot like resistance. Purpose-driven teachers may ask questions that seem extraneous or downright annoying, or they may want to engage in philosophical conversations that seem to be going nowhere. It may be tempting to dismiss their questions or concerns as simple resistance; however, if you really want to move purpose-driven teachers, you must take the time to address their concerns.

A perfect example of this occurred recently while I was conducting a series of workshops on rigor at a large high school. It was going well. Teachers were starting to develop rigorous unit plans and implement rigorous instructional strategies in their classrooms, and the differences were immediately apparent. Students were more engaged, the lessons were more focused on the learning objectives, and preliminary testing data had shown some upward movement in student achievement. I was feeling really good about the work we were doing when I visited the school midyear to conduct a series of troubleshooting sessions with small teams of teachers.

Then one teacher, Chris, raised his hand and asked me a question I was not expecting: "Why are we even focusing on rigor?"

We had spent the early part of the year conducting rigor workshops and lesson planning sessions with teachers. I thought we were beyond asking why, and I got a little defensive. I recounted the improvements that had been made in instruction, recited the small test-score gains already seen, and talked about the research basis for what we were doing. Chris was unmoved, offered a few counterpoints, and repeated his question: "Why rigor?"

Sensing the annoyance and restlessness of the other teachers and feeling my own frustration, I said, "Chris, I would love to get into a long philosophical conversation about 'why rigor,' but the purpose of this session is to troubleshoot problems you are having implementing rigorous instruction."

"But this *is* my problem with implementing rigorous instruction," he insisted. I realized that Chris was telling the truth: He really needed more help understanding the purpose of rigor in order to implement it. I arranged to meet with him later in the day, and continued with the troubleshooting session.

When I showed up at his classroom door that afternoon, he looked a little surprised to see me and said, "Hey, listen. It's no big deal. You don't have to do this."

"No, I want to," I lied, smiling bravely.

"OK." He didn't look convinced. "But I have to warn you: people think I'm ornery."

I laughed genuinely. That was *exactly* what I thought of him. "I'm not scared of you," I joked. "Go ahead. Hit me with your best shot."

Finally, a smile. "Look," Chris said, "it's just that every year, we get caught up in a new fad. Last year it was RTI. Two years ago, it was differentiated instruction. Now, it's rigor. I've had enough. I'm not doing anything else unless I'm convinced it will make a difference to my kids. I don't have time to jump on every bandwagon that comes my way."

We began a discussion of what rigor really is and how important it is that all students learn to think in highly rigorous ways. Instead of quoting him research or recounting data, I talked about rigor from a philosophical perspective. We touched on challenges facing 21st century learners, the lives his students led outside school, and his own goals and ideals. It was a great conversation.

A few weeks later Chris e-mailed me saying he was trying some of the rigorous instructional strategies I'd shared and was experiencing some success, but he had more questions. We exchanged a few more philosophical e-mails about the "bigger picture" of rigor, and it was enough to keep him motivated. By the end of the year, he had made tremendous progress toward planning and delivering more rigorous lessons, although he still needed to engage in those philosophical conversations before he'd take each new step. It was what Chris needed to keep moving forward.

Teachers who need purpose need to believe that what they are being asked to do matters, and they need to understand how it matters before they can get going. Once they understand the purpose, they will often take a new initiative or strategy and extend it far beyond what you imagined. There are specific ways to respond to purpose-driven teachers' sources of resistance (see Figure 5.3) and specific types of support to provide, namely, a connection to the big picture, explanation, freedom to set goals, and opportunity for inquiry and exploration.

A Connection to the Big Picture

The idea here is to help these teachers link the larger goals of the institution with their personal identity and sense of purpose. Spend time helping teachers connect what they are being asked to do to the greater vision

Figure 5.3   Responding to Purpose-Driven Teachers'
                      Sources of Resistance

Source	Message	Response
Limiting beliefs	"My work does not matter."	Show teachers how their work matters to students and to the success of the organization. Use nested praise to highlight the connection between their work and their outcomes.
Assumptions	"This project will be as pointless as the last one."	Demonstrate how the new project or initiative connects to the larger vision and purpose of the organization.
Fear	"I am afraid what I am doing won't matter."	Stress the connection between the teacher's work and the larger goals and purpose of the organization. Engage teachers in conversations about why they do what they do; articulate the institutional identity and how teachers fit into that identity.
Judgments	"This is stupid or pointless."	Explain the rationale behind a particular project or initiative. Engage teachers in conversations about the philosophical underpinnings, the proven results, and the research.
Obstacles	"The purpose of the organization conflicts with my own sense of purpose."	Clearly articulate the mission and vision of the organization and help teachers articulate their own vision and mission. Identify and emphasize similarities or connections.

of the school and district, and highlight for them their own role within it. It can also be really motivating for purpose-driven teachers to understand the identity of the organization. They feel connected—and more purposeful—when they understand "this is who we are and this is what we do." Finally, give these teachers a vision of what success looks like. Paint a compelling picture of what they, their students, and the school might achieve as a result of what it is you are asking them to do. Doing so will inspire them and help them contextualize their work within the larger vision of the school.

Explanation

Teachers who need purpose need to understand the rationale for any new initiative or requirement. Engage them in conversations focused on the purpose of a particular strategy or initiative. Answer their questions patiently; they need these conversations in order to become motivated and to understand what is expected of them. Once they understand the rationale, even if they don't agree with it, they will likely be able to move forward because they understand what it is you are trying to accomplish and why you have selected this particular approach. Often, once they understand your rationale, these teachers will offer suggestions, improvements, or tweaks that will enhance the initiative and better help you reach your purpose.

Freedom to Set Goals

Let teachers set their own professional development goals for the year. I am not talking about requiring teachers to create their own professional development plans; this often becomes another form of compliance. Have conversations with teachers about what they want to accomplish and provide them with the time (and the commensurate support) they need to pursue their own professional goals.

Opportunity for Inquiry and Exploration

Teachers who need purpose benefit from having time to participate in teacher research or involvement in a teacher inquiry group. Give teachers opportunities to explore or establish a research base for their practice, consider philosophical questions around education, read widely in the field, and reflect on the implications of their inquiry on their own practice. Nest any praise in terms of the purpose, vision, and mission of the organization. As teachers progress, give them positive feedback that helps them see their progress in light of the wider vision for themselves, their students, and the school.

 Checkpoint Summary

*Build the will of **purpose-driven** teachers by helping them understand what is being asked of them and how and why it matters.*

TOOLS FOR WILL DEVELOPMENT	RESULTING IN
A connection to the big picture	Increased optimism and more emotional investment in schoolwide initiatives
Explanation	Clarity on expectations, increased motivation, and (often) new ideas that will benefit others on staff
Freedom to set goals	Reassurance that they will be able to improve themselves in ways that matter to them and to the organization
Opportunity for inquiry and exploration	Increased engagement and a sense that they are involved in important work that will support the school's mission

Building Will in Belonging-Driven Teachers

Teachers motivated by a sense of belonging need to know that they matter to others. Connecting to others and establishing and tending relationships are very important to them. If the relationships are broken and they feel disconnected from their colleagues, their leaders, or their students, these teachers can quickly lose motivation. You must establish a relationship. If you just walk into their classrooms and start giving them feedback, they may resist any changes you ask them to make, not because they disagree with the change but because they feel that you are making suggestions without first getting to know them.

Ms. Ellis—Louise—was a very difficult teacher; in addition to being unpleasant to students, she was mildly insulting to her colleagues. Because she was a low-will/high-skill teacher, she technically met evaluative standards during all her formal observations, but she was a bully to her students and colleagues, and that was a problem.

My first approach to dealing with Louise was to come down hard on her every time I received a phone call from a parent or complaint from a student. If she wanted to be a bully, I'd show her what a bully could really do. I called her into my office, I used all of the power of my position to try to intimidate her, and I made it clear that she would be happier working somewhere else. This approach backfired. She called the union and demanded a union representative at every meeting. She trashed me in the staff lounge to anyone who would listen. And instead of treating students and colleagues more nicely, she became even sneakier in her meanness.

After several months of doing battle with Louise and seeing things only get worse, I suddenly made a connection between my relationship with this teacher and the relationship I had with one of my most difficult students, Keisha (see Jackson, 2009). The harder I came down on Keisha, the worse things got. It was when I started where Keisha was and established a relationship with her that I was able to reach her and help her move forward. I decided to try the same approach with Louise. The next time I visited her classroom, I found something to compliment. The next time I saw her in the hall, I asked her about her weekend rather than glaring at her and wishing she were gone. I made a point to stop by Louise's classroom in between classes and chat. I tried to get to know her as a person instead of simply seeing her as a problem.

Although Louise was suspicious at first, it wasn't long before she relaxed and welcomed my short visits. In fact, she began to show me pictures of her children and recommend books she thought I might like. However, Louise was still being mean to her students and colleagues. When I got the next complaint from a parent, I wasn't sure quite what to say to Louise. If I fussed or scolded her, she would defend her behavior and demand a union representative; then I would write her up, and she would grudgingly apologize to the student and the parent . . . and find even more subtle ways to exact her revenge on the student and on me. No one would win. Back to square one.

I knew that Louise was a technically skilled teacher and believed that if she could foster better relationships with the students, she had the potential to be a master teacher. I decided to try a different strategy.

It began with me visiting Louise in her classroom after school. I mentioned to her that I was having a hard day. I had gotten a call from a student's mother that morning, I explained, and what I had heard was really troubling. I told Louise that the student had answered a question during a class discussion the previous day. Evidently, he gave the wrong answer, because when he finished, his teacher said, "Do the world a favor and don't breed."

Louise's face darkened as she realized that I was talking about her.

I went on. "The mother said that her son was so embarrassed—the other children laughed at him. He couldn't sleep the entire night, and he's been throwing up. He couldn't even come to school today because he's so worked up."

Louise started to defend herself. "But I didn't mean anything by it!" she insisted. "I was just joking."

I could tell that she was getting reading to assume her traditional defensive position, gearing up to do battle. But I was about to change the plan.

"Your joke really hurt him, Louise," I said softly. "He thinks that you think he's stupid."

I let those last words hang in the air for a few moments. What I *didn't* do this time was berate Louise for being cruel or threaten to write her up or even demand that she apologize. It was hard not to, because I was angry with her. It was also hard to try to like her in that moment, because I cannot stand a bully. Louise braced herself for the tirade she was expecting . . . but it didn't come. And slowly, her face began to soften.

"I didn't mean to make him feel that way," she finally said. "I didn't think it through."

I nodded. "How are you going to fix this?"

"I don't know," she said. "What do you think I should do?"

We talked through the situation. Louise decided to call the student's mother to apologize, and she went on to apologize to the student in front of the entire class. She even engaged the class in a really interesting conversation about how words can wound and led them in a pledge to "be more careful with our words."

Louise was still mean from time to time. She still grated on her colleagues' nerves. But when she did, we were able to reach her and help her change her behavior—not through traditional disciplinary leadership tools but through the relationships we had established with her. When Louise felt liked, felt heard, and felt engaged as a colleague rather than scolded as a child, she was reachable.

For teachers who need belonging, the relationship comes first. If you don't first establish the relationship, they cannot hear your concerns about problems with their practice or your suggestions and solutions. If a teacher's primary will driver is belonging, start with the relationship and connect with the teacher first. Then and only then can you move that teacher's will. In addition to specifically addressing the reasons they may resist (see Figure 5.4), you can also take action to foster a sense of belonging for teachers who need it through *personal connection, merited praise,* and *community connection.*

Figure 5.4   Responding to Belonging-Driven Teachers'
Sources of Resistance

Source	Message	Response
Limiting beliefs	"I don't fit in."	Help teachers recognize and understand their role on their teams and in the organization. Show them how they contribute to the overall goals of the school.
Assumptions	"They won't like me." "I won't like them."	Work to overcome teachers' self-defense mechanisms by honoring the uniqueness of each individual in your school. Show teachers that you appreciate them individually and their important contributions to the school community.
Fear	"I am afraid I am not likable."	Establish relationships with teachers first before giving them negative feedback; phrase positive and negative feedback in terms of teachers' instructional decisions rather than personal characteristics.
Judgments	"That person doesn't like me."	Shift teachers' focus from whether or not they are liked to how they add to the school community; focus on their current or potential contributions.
Obstacles	"I cannot work with the people I've been asked to work with."	Manage interpersonal conflicts before they have a chance to escalate. Rearrange teams as needed so teachers can work productively together.

Personal Connection

Teachers who need belonging need to feel that you see them, that you like them, and that you respect them. Work on building a personal relationship with these teachers. You don't have to become their best friend, but you do need to help them feel that you see and appreciate them as an individual rather than just another employee. Teachers motived by belonging also want to know *how* they belong. Help them see what their role is in the overall school and how their role connects to other roles in the building.

Merited Praise

Often we forget to share positive feedback and praise with teachers who are "doing their jobs." Take time to offer praise to teachers, even for things that they should be doing anyway. Merited praise can be a powerful motivator for teachers who need belonging.

Community Connection

Teachers who need belonging want to be a part of something. Articulate for teachers that "we are a school that cares about children" or "we are a community of lifelong learners." By using "we" language and defining specifically the mores of the school community, you give teachers who need belonging a sense that they are included in the community and that they have a role to play in the success of that community. It's also important to remember that belonging-driven teachers need to collaborate with others in order to generate their best ideas and achieve to their potential. By arranging opportunities to collaborate with others, you help these teachers feel connected and you put them in a situation where they are motivated to do their best work

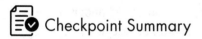 Checkpoint Summary

Build the will of **belonging-driven** teachers by stressing their value as individuals and as part of the whole.

TOOLS FOR WILL DEVELOPMENT	RESULTING IN
Personal connection	Increased engagement in the work of the school and increased investment in new initiatives and district mandates
Merited praise	A sense of validation and increased confidence
Community connection	A renewed sense of the importance of their contributions and motivation to do their best work

Back to Ms. McKay

After that meeting with Mr. Williams and Andrea, I spent the next few visits to the school observing Alison McKay more closely. I noticed that although she really was a good teacher, there were times when she would unintentionally sabotage her effectiveness. Sometimes it was an inappropriate attempt to "be cool" during instruction by using slang or making pop culture references that weren't quite connected to the lesson. Other times, she would try to engage with her students as if she was their age or attempt to join personal conversations between students. The students reported to me during one of my focus groups that they found her behavior "strange" and "lame." They wanted their teacher to act like a teacher.

With her colleagues, Ms. McKay was even more inept. She would brag about a lesson she created, and during group planning, she would talk mostly about herself, her classroom, and her successes while shooting down anyone else's suggestions. Although Andrea, the instructional coach, attempted to get Ms. McKay more involved by inviting her to present at a staff meeting, that presentation managed to insult all the teachers in attendance, as Ms. McKay scolded half the teachers for not regularly using a strategy she shared and the other half for using it incorrectly.

When I considered Ms. McKay, I saw a teacher who was desperate to be liked but didn't know how to be likable. She preened under praise and crumbled under criticism. She compensated for her insecurity by bragging and trying to be "cool." Once I shared my observations with Mr. Williams, we settled on a plan.

For a month, he and Andrea focused their feedback solely on Ms. McKay's lessons, providing praise for what went well and offering suggestions on ways to improve what didn't. Because she was a relatively high-skill teacher and quite effective in the classroom, they had a lot to praise; because she was so hungry for praise, she eagerly accepted and implemented their suggestions. As she began to trust their feedback, Mr. Williams and Andrea began to show her how to navigate interpersonal relationships by coaching her prior to her team meetings. They gave her strategies for how to contribute without bragging, how to listen with openness, and how to provide positive feedback to others. Over time, they were able to help her have better interpersonal relationships with her students.

The lesson here is that a will solution is the only way to solve a will problem. By matching your leadership response to teachers' individual will-building needs, you can salvage a good teacher, help an ineffective teacher become effective, and get every teacher moving toward mastery.

YES, BUT . . .
What if I don't have the will to move someone else's will?

There are times when, even though you understand what a teacher's primary will driver is and have a plan for moving his will, your own will is depleted and you don't want to invest any more time or energy in that teacher. What do you do when your own will has gone?

The primary will drivers work for you as well as for others, so the first step is to understand what your primary will driver is. Use **Tool 3** in the Appendix to help figure it out. For instance, if your will driver is mastery, you may tend to try to motivate others using mastery. But if mastery is not their will driver, they will remain unmotivated, further frustrating you. Take a clear look at yourself and learn to check any tendency to focus on your own currencies rather than the currencies of your teachers.

Next, use your primary will driver to *motivate yourself to motivate others*. When I am having a hard time motivating a reluctant teacher or I just don't feel like feeding a teacher's particular will driver, I focus on my own need for mastery. Then I figure out how I am going to master motivating that teacher who is driving me nuts. Before long, it isn't about the teacher; it's about meeting my own need for mastery while meeting the teacher's needs. Win-win.

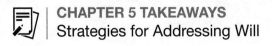

CHAPTER 5 TAKEAWAYS
Strategies for Addressing Will

IF TEACHERS NEED . . .	GIVE THEM . . .
Autonomy	• Several suggestions or recommendations from which they can choose • Choices about time, task, technique, team, and territory • Descriptive rather than prescriptive feedback in noncontrolling language that implies that they always have a choice
Mastery	• Deliberate practice with clear goals and immediate feedback • Novelty • Challenge • Frequent growth-oriented feedback
Purpose	• Opportunities to set their own professional learning goals • Reasons behind new initiatives, requests, and suggestions • Opportunities to participate in teacher inquiry • A clear vision for the organization and an understanding of their own role in it • Nested praise
Belonging	• Nonevaluative, casual conversation about teaching • Access to you and to others who can help them • Opportunities to work with others • Strategies for forging positive relationships with colleagues and students

6

PUTTING IT ALL TOGETHER

What looks like a people problem is often a situation problem. And, no matter what your role is, you've got some control over the situation.

—Chip Heath and Dan Heath, Switch

It was 7:00 a.m. when I got the panicked call from Beth, a principal, about Mr. Schulman, a teacher at her school. "Danny called in sick again today—he left a message on the school answering machine. He called in sick again, and he doesn't have any more leave!"

Here we go again, I thought. I was working with Beth's K–8 school to help create structures that would set her teachers and students up for success, but most of our conversations lately revolved around one teacher: Danny Schulman. He was ineffective in the classroom and also struggled with professionalism—calling in sick without securing a substitute, using up all of his leave, leaving work before the end of his duty day, and telling parents and sometimes even students that he really didn't want to be there. His lack of motivation and his unprofessional attitude were wearing on other teachers who faced their own struggles to remain motivated. It was certainly wearing on Beth; dealing with problems related to Mr. Schulman was becoming a job unto itself.

A week later, Beth put Mr. Schulman on an official improvement plan. She outlined the behaviors she expected him to improve, required that he turn in weekly lesson plans, told him that he was out of leave and therefore had to be at school each day, detailed the extent of his duties and his duty day, and promised unannounced formal observations of his class to check on his progress. Mr. Schulman received his plan without a word, but as soon as he left Beth's office he began to complain to the other teachers. Beth was out to get him, he said. He was going to look for another job. However, he complied with the stipulations of the plan, dutifully submitting lesson plans each week, showing up for work on time, and staying in his office after school until the end of his duty day. When Beth came to his class, he immediately got up and began to teach the students; the moment she left, he returned to his seat and resumed his prior activity: surfing the Internet looking at job postings.

By the end of the school year, Mr. Schulman had performed all of the improvement steps on his improvement plan, but he had not improved at all. Beth attempted to terminate him, but Mr. Schulman appealed to the school board, presenting his improvement plan and evidence that he had faithfully met every one of its formal requirements. The paperwork was all there. Beth had no choice but to renew Mr. Schulman's contract for the following year.

You could probably tell your own version of this story. We've all heard about teachers who are clearly underperforming but who remain in the classroom because of "the way things work." We blame the unions or the bureaucracy, or we shrug wearily and accept it as all a part of the game. You win some; you lose some. When facing ineffective teachers, we are taught, we need to work diligently to remove them from the classroom. We start building a case and make sure that our *i*'s are dotted and our *t*'s are crossed. We offer resources and create improvement plans in order to demonstrate that we gave the teacher every opportunity to improve. If we gather the right evidence and get the right paperwork in order, we get to remove the teacher from the classroom and hire a better teacher.

But what if there were a different way to deal with ineffective teachers? What if you could improve teacher performance *and* attitude? What if, in fact, you could get all of your teachers focused on and moving toward mastery?

Building a Mastery-Focused Environment

It's inspiring to be in a school where every teacher is working toward mastery. But masterful teaching doesn't happen by accident: It's a choice each teacher must make. The purpose of leading in a way that honors teachers' will and skill is to help teachers choose mastery every day. It really is as simple as creating an environment focused on mastery that feeds people's will and skill needs. It really is as simple as creating the right kind of support and practice.

One of the reasons this can be hard to believe is the *fundamental attribution error*, which is "our inclination to attribute people's behavior to the way they are rather than the situation they are in" (Heath & Heath, 2010, p. 180). However, it is the situation, not some immutable character flaw, that produces most behavior—and situations are infinitely easier to change than someone's character. If you encounter what seems like an intractable character problem, you often can change that person by changing the situation the person is in. If you shape the path to mastery the right way, you can get a lot more people on it.

The other really good news about the fundamental attribution error is that we were wrong: Most teaching behavior—good or bad—is *not* the result of some inherent character trait. Good teaching is not innate; bad teaching is not immutable. It doesn't take a personality transplant to turn a "bad" teacher into an effective teacher. By changing the situation, you can change a teacher's effectiveness.

The fundamental attribution error tells us that environments are more powerful than we think or, rather, more powerful than what we want to believe. A good environment can make an ineffective teacher better, and a bad environment can make a good teacher worse. So every detail matters—from how the teachers plan lessons to how they start class to their professional development activities.

You must keep your staff focused on what matters; otherwise, they will focus on what matters to *them*. How do you shape this environment?

Set the Vision

What does masterful teaching look like in this building? What does it mean in terms of our students? What will masterful teaching help us accomplish as a school?

Once you've articulated your vision, charge your teachers with figuring out how they will personally help move the school toward the vision. Be sure to engage their primary will drivers in the process (see Chapters 4 and 5). Reconsider or reshape the rules of engagement in your professional culture based on teacher feedback to make it easier for teachers to move the school toward the vision. Make sure you provide differentiated, developmental, and deliberate support for teacher skill to keep them moving toward that vision (see Chapters 2 and 3).

Establish Structures to Track Progress Toward the Vision

Engage teachers in conversations about their practice, what mistakes they are making, and, most important, how they are learning from those mistakes. Help teachers develop a clear plan with effective strategies for accomplishing the vision—and maintaining the vision once they've achieved it. Show respect for their efforts, and praise their strategies rather than their personal characteristics. When there are setbacks, discuss the mistakes and help teachers learn from them.

A mastery-focused environment is powerful. It allows teachers to make mistakes; indeed, it makes making mistakes a part of the process. Although mistakes are inevitable, most teachers hide their mistakes because they don't want to affect your perception of them and their teaching. But making mistakes is a part of the learning and growth process; by establishing a climate in which mistakes are discussed openly and without judgment, teachers can deal with their mistakes and learn from them. In the process, you make making mistakes a lot less likely.

A mastery-focused environment is also one where every teacher is personally invested. Your entire teaching staff is tasked with figuring out how they fit into the overall vision. How they invest aligns with their will drivers and skills. This type of environment keeps masterful teaching at the forefront of everyone's thoughts. It cultivates a long-term investment in mastery and has supports in place to ensure that every teacher gets there.

Every Teacher on the Pathway to Mastery

Great teaching happens on purpose. It's deliberate. Master teachers are masterful because they decided to be and they did the work required to get there. There are things that you can do to help all your teachers make the decision to strive for and ultimately achieve masterful teaching. Your approach to inspiring and encouraging teachers to commit to mastery, however, differs by the type of teacher you encounter (see Chapter 1).

Low-Will/Low-Skill Teachers

The difficulty in working with low-will/low-skill teachers is knowing where to start. Do you work on their will or work on their skill, or must you juggle both simultaneously? The answer depends on whether low will is the reason that they are low skill or low skill is the reason that they are low will. Teasing this out isn't easy. It can take some digging to get to the root of their ineffectiveness.

One way to determine the root cause of teachers' low will and skill is to engage them in conversations about why they went into teaching to begin with and their first days in the classroom. In as nonthreatening a way as possible, ask them to describe their early teaching experiences and listen for evidence of some preliminary motivation or preliminary skill. In many cases, low-will/low-skill teachers started out wanting to be good, but they did not receive the support they needed, and so they never got better. Over time, they got frustrated and gave up. Other times, these teachers went into teaching for the wrong reasons (e.g., summers off or they couldn't get a "better" job), meaning they were never really motivated to get good. Listen to their stories. If you can determine which came first, the low skill or the low will, then start working on that area first.

Another approach is to start with will. If you can ignite the desire to get better in these teachers, you can get them on the path to mastery. Pay attention to their primary will driver (see Chapter 4). Once you've determined what motivates them, use their primary will driver to get them motivated (see Chapter 5). If they are driven by mastery, try to set these teachers up for success. If they are driven by purpose, try to reconnect them to their sense of purpose, or appeal to their ideals as a way to get them started. If they are driven by autonomy, provide some preliminary autonomy by loosening up on one of the five T's (see p. 94), with the promise of more autonomy as they improve. If they need belonging, work at getting them connected to their colleagues and establishing a better relationship with them yourself. When working with low-will/low-skill teachers, rather than focusing on raising their will in general, I focus on raising their will regarding a specific task. Once they become motivated about something specific, they are more likely to become motivated about their work in general.

The key danger when working with these teachers is that you will give up too soon. Low-will/low-skill teachers are experts at waiting you out. It may seem as if you are not making progress for months, and you may find yourself getting frustrated and resorting to coercion as a way to get these teachers moving. But coercion is exhausting; you end up working harder than the teacher, and low-will/low-skill teachers are happy to let you take on the ownership and the lion's share of the work for their improvement. What you really want is cooperation, which takes more time and more skill to achieve. You have to manage your frustration and keep your focus on the overall goal of mastery for every teacher. Over time, it will be easier for these teachers to cooperate with you than to continue to resist you, especially when they realize that there is no waiting you out.

Another powerful tool you have when working with low-will/high-skill teachers is the power of momentum. Start on getting your most willing teachers moving first. They will create momentum, a gravitational pull that will make your work less difficult when you turn your attention to your more resistant teachers.

Finally, if you want to get these teachers on the path to mastery, shape the path itself. Create an instructional environment where doing the right thing is much easier and doing the wrong thing is much harder. Often, low-will/low-skill teachers aren't defiant; they are just taking the path of least resistance. In creating a mastery-focused environment, you are also creating a teaching environment where it is much easier or even natural to do the things that are best for students.

YES, BUT . . .
I'm trying with these teachers, but we're getting nowhere!

The key to working with low-will/low-skill teachers is to be patient. It may take a while to get these teachers started or to build momentum. Many leaders give up too soon and resort to coercive leadership tactics. This will get you compliance but not real cooperation from low-will/low-skill teachers. If you really want every teacher in your building moving toward mastery, you are going to have to strategically invest in these teachers. This doesn't mean settling for inertia in the name of patience; it means that you need to focus on incremental movement until you build momentum and to hold teachers accountable in a way that doesn't paralyze them.

Consider the example of Terry, a middle school principal, who helped a low-will/low-skill teacher show up for team meetings on time simply by switching the meeting location to the teacher's classroom. Without a single threat, "courageous conversation," or letter to a file, he set up a situation where this teacher, who had been chronically late to meetings or prone to "forgetting" and not showing up at all, was able to achieve perfect attendance. Then there is Sheila, an instructional coach, who helped her low-will/low-skill elementary school teachers develop professional portfolios. She set aside 20 minutes of every staff meeting for "portfolio time," where teachers were expected to work on their portfolios, and she and the administrators worked with them. This provided low-skill teachers the support they needed and low-will teachers with an environmental incentive to complete the work.

Now consider your own instructional environment. Are there aspects of the current culture that make it easier to get away with not moving toward mastery? Are there adjustments you can make to make it easier for low-will/low-skill teachers to improve? Often by just tweaking your environment, you can get these teachers on the path to mastery.

High-Will/Low-Skill Teachers

High-will/low-skill teachers want to get better but struggle with the how. Thus, the challenge is to improve their skill while maintaining their will. Again, you need to start by determining their will driver. This, along with an understanding of the root causes of their low skill, will help you determine which combination of professional development opportunities will best help them.

Choose professional development opportunities that will address the root cause of their low skill while simultaneously maintaining their high will. For example, suppose you have a high-will/low-skill teacher at the apprentice level (see Chapter 2) who struggles with effective lesson planning. As she works on developing more effective plans, she will need a lot of prescriptive feedback. Tailor the feedback to accommodate her primary will driver. If it's mastery, she will need prescriptive feedback that affirms that you believe that she is ultimately capable of reaching mastery. If her driver is purpose, then she needs prescriptive feedback that reinforces or is reinforced by her mission and values. If she is driven by autonomy, she will need prescriptive feedback that focuses on the choices she is making and offers her options for how she can respond. If she is driven by belonging, she will need prescriptive feedback that maintains a connection and relationship with you, her colleagues, and her students. It's the same feedback, but how you deliver that feedback can make all the difference.

Let's say you have a teacher whose plans seem to just list the activities for the day rather than linking these to the standards or a mastery objective for students. Here's how you might couch the feedback for each will driver:

- *Mastery:* "I see that you have listed your activities for the day here in your plans, but what is it that you ultimately want students to accomplish through these activities? What standard do you want them to master by the end of your lesson?"
- *Purpose:* "What is the purpose of the activities that you have listed here? In other words, what is your goal for the day's lesson? How does that connect with the larger goals for the unit as expressed in the standards? How can you communicate the purpose of the lesson activities to students in a way that they can understand?"

- *Autonomy:* "This is a great first draft. One area to work on is your objectives. Right now, they are more activities than they are goals for what students should know or be able to do by the end of the lesson. Would you tweak the mastery objectives to focus on what students need to know or be able to do? For example, you have your choice of these unit standards, and you can choose to focus on any one of them. I am happy to help you craft a few objectives if you like, or you can work on your own and I could give you feedback on the revised draft."

- *Belonging:* "One thing I noticed about your lesson plan is that it lists activities instead of objectives. So although I know what your students will do during the lesson, I still don't know what the overall goal is. Would you like to work together to come up with a few objectives for your lesson that are more focused on what students will know or be able to do at the end of your lesson?"

Couching feedback in a way that feeds teachers' primary will driver helps them be more receptive to that feedback. By shaping your support for improving skill in a way that also maintains will, you can help these teachers put in the long, hard work they need to improve and make it less likely that they will give up along the way.

High-Will/High-Skill Teachers

High-will/high-skill teachers can present a challenge in that they are already motivated and are already highly skilled. It can be tempting to just let them do their own thing. If you are strapped for time, you may end up devoting your energies to teachers who need more help and ignoring these teachers altogether. But this is a mistake. These are the best teachers in your building, and if you want to keep them that way, you need to make sure that they remain motivated and challenged; otherwise, they will seek that motivation and challenge elsewhere, in another school or in another role, usually *outside* the classroom.

You will need to take the time to engage purpose-driven high-will/high-skill teachers in conversations about the vision and mission of the school and their own values. Share your values with these teachers as well so that they can clearly understand why you lead the way that you lead. Engage mastery-driven teachers in conversations about the work of

YES, BUT . . .
With all my other responsibilities, I just can't justify devoting tons of time to high-will/high-skill teachers. And I don't really need to; they're already doing a great job!

If you are strapped for time, it is more important to maintain your high-will/high-skill teachers' will than their skill. If you can keep these teachers motivated and if you have opportunities for growth and collaboration in place and built into the way that your school operates, you don't have to directly provide these teachers with professional development. They will seek it themselves and get it from one another.

Remember, though, that no matter how self-motivated they are, high-will/high-skill teachers still need external support. If you don't provide that support, mastery-driven teachers may start to slack off, purpose-driven teachers may become cynical, belonging-driven teachers may start to withdraw, and autonomous teachers may "go rogue" and start focusing on goals that don't mesh with your vision for the school. Devote your efforts with high-will/high-skill teachers to sustaining their will over time.

teaching itself and new innovations or theories you have read about. Talk to them about what good teaching looks like to keep them focused on the goal of mastery for every teacher. Engage teachers driven by belonging in conversations that keep them connected to you; put them in situations where they can stay connected to their colleagues rather than isolating them. Maintain the delicate balance for autonomous teachers between their freedom to choose how they teach and their accountability to the students, their colleagues, and the school system.

Low-Will/High-Skill Teachers

Working with low-will/high-skill teachers is challenging because in most cases they are following the letter of the law. These teachers know how to pass an evaluation and have a range of effective teaching strategies. However, their teaching suffers because they are unwilling to fully commit to their craft. Maybe they are satisfied with performing just above average, or perhaps they are convinced that what they do is "good enough." It can be really hard to motivate teachers convinced that they don't need help.

The key to working with these teachers is to spend time observing them so that you can determine their will drivers. Then, figure out what obstacles are getting in the way of their commitment to improving, and remove those obstacles (see Chapter 3). Next, identify where they are on the master teacher trajectory and select professional development opportunities that best speak to their will drivers. For instance, if you encounter a low-will/high-skill teacher who is at the practitioner level and whom you know is driven by mastery, start by providing micropractice and evaluation. For another teacher driven by belonging, however, start with opportunities for collaboration. If a teacher is driven by purpose, start by offering opportunities for elaboration, and if the motivator is autonomy, start by offering opportunities for reflection and elaboration.

Another way to reach low-will/high-skill teachers is to engage them in conversations about their early teaching experiences. Ask them why they chose teaching as a career and what their first few years of teaching were like. Your goal is not only to establish rapport but also to understand what happened that sapped their will over time. Remember, most low-will/high-skill teachers developed their skill because, at some point, they had high will. If you can figure out what sapped that will, you will have powerful cues as to how to go about restoring it.

The hard part about working with low-will/high-skill teachers is that because these teachers have high skill, they may not feel that they need much skill development. If that is the case, they will resist your efforts to improve their skill and may even act as saboteurs in your building, undermining your overall efforts to promote professional development. Be careful here, and resist being drawn into power struggles. You need to remain steadfast and work on these teachers' will by leading them in ways that address their primary will driver. Low-will/high-skill teachers will often try your patience, but hold on. If you can reignite their enthusiasm for the work and help them move from low will/high skill to high will/high skill, the most resistant teachers in your building can become among the best on your staff.

Power Dynamics

One of the hardest things about building mastery in teachers is navigating the power dynamics.

If you are an instructional coach, you are tasked with helping teachers improve without the authority to do much if they resist your efforts. If you are an administrator, you have the opposite problem: You want to coach teachers to improve, but your authority may undermine your coaching efforts.

Although you must be aware of the power dynamics and how they play out in your school, you have a lot of control over whether they will actually get in the way of your work. The real key to keeping power dynamics from hurting your progress is to refuse to get into power struggles. Some teachers will attempt to engage you in these conflicts either overtly, by direct resistance, or covertly, by sabotaging your efforts. Either way, it is important that you don't get lured into this drama. Keep your eye on the goal: every teacher on the path to mastery.

If you are a coach, fellow teacher, team leader, or department head, you occupy two very nebulous roles—peer and coach—that are defined more by *what you're not* than by what you are. You are not quite a colleague and not quite a supervisor. It can be a difficult divide to navigate. Some teachers may resent your intrusion into their practice and see you as a proxy for the administration. Other teachers may wonder whether you really have anything to offer them, given that you are their professional peer. It is important to clarify your role as a coach up front and help teachers understand the purpose of coaching.

A coach can see you in ways that you cannot see yourself, offering a unique perspective to help you improve. One of the reasons even the greatest performers, athletes, and CEOs still submit to coaching even after they have reached the height of expertise is that they need an objective lens through which they can view their practice. Before coaches start dispensing advice or managing a teacher's work, they should provide feedback in a way that best meets the teacher's will and skill needs. Using reflective, facilitative, and coaching conversations can help teachers move their practice forward without getting ensnared in power dynamics.

If you are a principal or assistant principal, you also occupy two roles: supervisor and coach. You are there to help teachers grow and improve; on the other hand, you also evaluate their growth, monitor how well they do their job, and ultimately decide whether they "fit" your organization. The only way to navigate these power dynamics is to openly acknowledge them. Otherwise, your interactions with teachers will always maintain a veneer of civility layered over distrust and dishonesty as teachers attempt to hide their deficits in order to keep their jobs. Acknowledge the fact that you are both a helper and an evaluator, and distinguish between the two roles for teachers.

It is a careful balancing act. One way to help you maintain balance is to put structures in place that naturally distinguish between your two roles. Whenever you implement a new reform or strategy, structure the process in a way that helps manage the power dynamics but also gives teachers time to develop unhindered by the threat of observation. This four-stage process—explore, expect, evaluate, and extend—provides clearly defined roles but also flexibility and autonomy.

At the beginning of the process, announce and explain the new initiative. Then share with teachers how you will roll out the initiative school-wide. Specify the role teachers are expected to play and what role you will play—supervisor or coach—at each phase of the process. If you delineate roles at the very beginning of the process and stick to these roles throughout the process, you don't have to wrestle with the power dynamics. Teachers understand what is expected of them, and administrators have spelled out the purpose of their support at each stage of the process.

Stage 1: Explore (3–6 Weeks)

At the beginning of any new initiative, give teachers time to explore it and figure out how they will implement it in their classrooms. Provide initial professional development, and allow teachers the time and space to experiment with new strategies in their own classrooms. The expectation at this point is not perfect implementation; the expectation is that teachers will *attempt* the new instructional practices in their classrooms. During this time you may begin informal, nonevaluative supervisory walk-throughs to track teachers' progress schoolwide, identify areas of need, and look for exemplars of successful implementation. Use this time to develop your own proficiency in recognizing effective and ineffective practice, diagnose teacher will and skill, and use your diagnoses to plan how you will support teachers in the next phase of the process.

Stage 2: Expect (2–4 Weeks)

At this point, set a new expectation: Teachers will implement new practices consistently. They may not be perfect, but you should be able to see the target instructional practice in consistent use in every teacher's classroom.

Announce that you will be visiting classrooms, and share with teachers the rubric or tool you will use to collect data and provide feedback. Although these visits are not evaluative, they can prepare the way for the upcoming evaluation process. Explain what you will be looking for when you visit classrooms during the upcoming evaluation process, and give teachers time to understand the criteria. Use the walk-through process to look for evidence that teachers are implementing the target practices and to provide the appropriate feedback. Invite selected groups of teachers on collegial walk-throughs, and analyze the trends you are seeing in the classroom.

Use the data you collect to identify additional professional development and support needs schoolwide. Informally, give teachers individual feedback, making sure to be particularly specific with any teachers who are still not implementing the target instructional practices. Use strategic conversations to help your most resistant teachers understand that every teacher in the building is expected to implement the target instructional practices. Try to get to the source of their resistance, and use the strategies in Chapter 5 to overcome their resistance so that they can successfully implement the target practice. Document these conversations.

Stage 3: Evaluate (6–8 Weeks)

By this time, teachers have engaged in professional learning and practice, and they should be implementing the target instructional practice not only consistently but with quality. Now, your role shifts to an evaluative one.

Use informal and formal evaluation processes to monitor how well teachers are implementing the practices, provide formative and evaluative feedback, and hold teachers accountable. Although you should get to every teacher's classroom at least once during this process, it is a good idea to start with your most resistant teachers. Hold these teachers accountable for implementing the target instructional practice effectively. Follow up with low-skill and low-will teachers within two weeks in order to ensure that they are making progress. Don't let too much time pass between visits, or teachers will lose their momentum.

YES, BUT . . .
What if a teacher refuses to or doesn't improve, despite my best efforts?

Developing teacher will and skill is a significant investment. It is easy to get frustrated and revert to earlier behaviors of rewards and punishments, carrots and sticks. But what if you've used every tool in your leadership toolbox and still nothing's worked?

The process of getting rid of "bad" teachers requires a lot of time and energy. Even if you choose to invest this time and energy, there is no guarantee that your efforts will be successful. More important, spending your energy getting rid of "bad" teachers instead of developing better teachers means you are focused on the wrong goal. When you decide a teacher is beyond your help, when you give up on a teacher, you send the message that it is OK for some teachers to not reach mastery and that becoming a master teacher is beyond the reach of some. What's more, it is difficult if not impossible for teachers to give their best to students if they are simultaneously concerned about keeping their jobs. And it is nearly impossible for a teacher who is fighting with the school administration to choose mastery. Whereas coercive leadership tactics shift everyone's attention from teaching to the players in the situation, investing in great teaching keeps the focus firmly on the students.

During this time, you should also track student data to see what improvements students are making on key benchmarks. Look for correlations between these data and the change in teacher practice, and share this information with teachers so that they can see the difference the changes you have asked them to make are having on student achievement. This kind of success can build momentum, increase or sustain motivation, and solidify teacher buy-in.

Stage 4: Extend (Ongoing)

When all teachers are implementing the target instructional practices consistently and with quality, the next step is to help teachers extend their practice and continue to grow.

At this point, you will know where all of your teachers are in terms of their ability to implement the target instructional practices, and you will be able to provide individual support and feedback to extend their professional growth. This means toggling back and forth between your roles as evaluator and coach—continuing to hold teachers accountable and providing additional assistance for those who are still struggling. One way to make this easier is to enlist instructional coaches, department chairs, team leaders, lead teachers, or high-will/high-skill teachers to help with the coaching and focus on your role as evaluator.

The Professional Culture You Want

Teaching is not merely a set of behaviors; it is a way of thinking about learning. If you do not change a teacher's mindset, you cannot significantly change the way a teacher teaches. How you change a teacher's mindset makes all the difference.

Coercive leadership doesn't work. It may get you compliance but not cooperation. Instead, taking into account teachers' will and skill can help you help teachers choose mastery every time. In addition, you have to tweak the environment. By creating an environment that cultivates great teaching—one that puts mastery at the fore—you can help teachers choose the pathway to mastery. If you shape the path to mastery the right way, more teachers will choose it.

So what does this outcome look like? What does it look like when a leader balances teachers' will and skill needs to change the way that they think about teaching? What does it look like when leaders shape the path to make mastery more likely?

In one district where I was administrator, there was a mandate to make grading and reporting more accurately reflect the way that students learn. The grading policy we had disincentivized learning by promoting a fixed attitude toward achievement, and district leaders wanted to change the policy to give students more growth-oriented feedback. After carefully examining the research, engaging in months of conversation, considering the grading policies in exemplar districts, and looking at district data, those leaders announced a radical change to the district's grading and reporting policy. Unfortunately, they did this three weeks before the beginning of a new school year.

Our school-based leadership team believed in the changes, but we also knew that they were so drastic that teachers would have a difficult time adjusting. How could we support teacher will and skill to make the change as easy as possible?

Two parts of the policy would be especially difficult for teachers to implement. The first was the requirement that teachers offer students opportunities for reassessment. Not only could we expect philosophical objections, but we could expect practical concerns about how to manage the time needed to create, administer, and grade these assessments. The second part of the policy was that teachers would no longer be allowed to give students zeros. If teachers used a 100-point scale, the lowest grade they could give to students was 50 percent, even if the student never turned in the assignment. Some teachers, we knew, would find this especially galling and might interpret it as mandating grade inflation.

We trained team leaders and department chairs to facilitate discussions among the staff. After introducing the new policy at a general staff meeting on the teachers' first day back, we gave teachers several opportunities over the following few days to discuss the policy in their subject-alike groups and interdisciplinary teams. We allowed teachers to determine how they would implement the new grading policy, by discipline and by grade level. This process gave teachers time to digest the policy and accept it—and time and tools to figure out how they would implement it.

We also looked for ways to make implementing the policy much easier. We rearranged the master schedule to build in 30 minutes each day for reteaching and retesting without sacrificing class time or planning time. To help teachers address the additional test-preparation and grading responsibilities, we showed teachers how to use their current assessments to make *A* and *B* versions of the same test, arranged for teachers to exchange teacher-created assessments with other teachers in the district, and showed teachers how to create Scantron versions of their retests to reduce their grading load. To address concerns about grade inflation and students gaming the system, we added a tweak to the policy. Any student could retake a test, with two caveats. First, "retakers" would have to engage in some sort of nonpunitive, corrective action designed to help them learn what they demonstrated they hadn't learned on the test—and this would be determined by the teacher. We gave them several examples of appropriate corrective actions such as reteaching sessions, online tutorials, and test corrections. The second caveat was that students could retake any test used for formative assessment up until the date of the scheduled summative assessment.

At first, many teachers implemented the policy without really believing in it. But because we made implementing the policy easier and integrated it into our culture, teachers complied and did so with some degree of proficiency. Teachers implemented the new policy not necessary because they believed in it but because it was now a part of the culture. By helping them build skill and shaping the environment, we bought ourselves time to work on their will.

Their will didn't change for several months, and then only after they started to see the new policy working. I remember one teacher who had been adamantly against the policy stopping by my office a few months after school began and saying, "I still hate this new grading policy, but I have to admit that my students are understanding more and performing better in my class." By the end of the year, she was on board. Five years later, the "new" grading policy is such a part of the learning culture of the school that teachers report they would not have it any other way.

You won't always change will right away, but you can change will over time—if you equip teachers with the appropriate skills and if you shape the environment to make implementing the new policy or teaching approach or initiative easy to do.

In the example I've shared, allowing teachers to create a grading policy that fit their subject matter, grade level, and teaching style fed their need for autonomy. Letting them plan together in grade- and subject-alike groups fed their need for belonging. Giving them strategies to help them implement the new policy and providing plenty of job-embedded training fed their need for mastery. Explaining the philosophy behind the new initiative and engaging teachers in philosophical discussions fed their need for purpose. In addition to facilitating their skill, it fed their will.

This is the power of leading with both skill and will in mind. It helps you reach your goals in a way that honors your teachers. It helps you serve your students better by giving them better teachers. It's not always pretty, but it's powerful. It helps you navigate difficult or tricky situations in a way that supports your teachers and brings out the best in them. And it brings out the best in you, too.

FOR YOUR . . .	SHAPE THE ENVIRONMENT	SHAPE YOUR LEADERSHIP APPROACH	MANAGE THE POWER DYNAMICS
Low-Will/Low-Skill Teachers	• Create an instructional environment where it is easier for teachers to do the right thing and harder for them to do the wrong thing (or nothing at all).	• Engage teachers in conversations to determine which is more prevalent, low will or low skill, and start there first. • If in doubt, address will first and then skill.	• Focus on building cooperation rather than defaulting to coercive leadership techniques. • Give teachers time to cooperate but start with these teachers first once you shift to evaluative feedback.
Low-Will/High-Skill Teachers	• Develop environmental cues that feed their primary will driver.	• Build will and leverage momentum.	• Clarify leadership roles throughout the process. • Resist the urge to engage in power struggles.
High-Will/Low-Skill Teachers	• Incorporate making and learning from mistakes into the instructional culture.	• Build skill while maintaining will.	• Clarify leadership roles throughout the process. • Give teachers time to practice before shifting to more evaluative feedback.
High-Will/High-Skill Teachers	• Keep the focus on how mastery directly affects the school vision and goals.	• Sustain will by continuing to invest in these teachers. • Allow them to choose how they will improve their skill, and provide appropriate supports.	• Maintain high will and skill by not abusing your power. Allow these teachers plenty of freedom, and provide informal leadership opportunities.

CONCLUSION:
EVERY TEACHER, EVERY LEADER

Look at the world around you. It may seem like an immovable, implacable place. It is not. With the slightest push—in just the right place—it can be tipped.
—*Malcolm Gladwell, The Tipping Point*

I recently read a story about a teacher who threw a chair at his students. When asked to explain what happened, the teacher said that he had been out drinking the night before and had a hangover; he threw the chair to make the students be quiet because he had a headache. A story like this challenges my belief that every teacher can become a master teacher.

I struggled with this idea as I wrote this book. How can I insist that every teacher can become a master teacher when there are teachers out there who are throwing chairs (or worse) at their students? How can I insist we take the time to develop every teacher when students' lives and futures are at stake? What answers do I have for leaders who are tasked with supervising these teachers? What can I tell coaches who are charged with making these teachers better?

Supporting Choice, Leading Change

The thing is, any teacher *can* become a master teacher . . . but not every teacher will. Ultimately, every teacher has a choice. As an instructional leader, you can work to make choosing mastery more attractive. You can mitigate or remove the barriers to teachers' will and help teachers develop increased skill. You can create a rigorous and supportive instructional climate where good teaching can thrive. And yet, even in the most ideal of working conditions, some teachers will still choose not to work toward mastery. Some teachers will insist on being mediocre or refuse to help certain students or have inappropriate sexual relationships with minors. Some teachers will hurl furniture. As much as we would like for every teacher to choose to work toward mastery, some teachers, despite your best efforts, will choose otherwise.

Does that mean that you give up on teachers? No. Most teachers *will* choose to work toward mastery if they have the right support. Some will stick at it long enough to achieve mastery, but others will get distracted along the way or choose to pursue other careers instead, and that's OK. The important thing is that while they are with you, they are on the path toward mastery. Again, teachers always have a choice. The instructional leader's charge is to never underestimate what teachers are capable of achieving . . . and to make choosing mastery an attractive and attainable option.

Here's a look back at how we do that, along with some final caveats and tips.

Make Sure That You Differentiate

It isn't fair to ask a novice to practice at the same level as a master teacher. They have different levels of skill. Practice opportunities need to be matched to each teacher's current skill level and move teachers to the next level of skill over time. A novice will not leap to the level of a master teacher as a result of a single workshop or coaching session, no matter how well designed. With the right kind of practice and support they'll get there, but it will take time. By the same token, master teachers need new challenges that are matched to their skill level if they are to continually grow and sustain their will over time. Every teacher in your school should be developed, not just the underperforming teachers or the "good" teachers. Differentiate your approach to best fit your teachers' needs.

Remember Your Goal

The presence or absence of a certain teaching behavior does not indicate the quality of the lesson—whether students are learning does. Effective teaching is much more than mastering a discrete set of knowledge and skills. It's about developing a mindset, an internal voice that helps teachers plan effective lessons, solve problems on the spot, and ultimately make the right decision for every student every day. Your goal is not to make perfect teachers who conform to every line on your evaluation system but to develop master teachers who make good decisions informed by their own expertise and guided by the goals of the institution.

Remember That Teaching Is Hard

Although it's common to see ineffective teachers labeled as "struggling," that label is misleading. Most ineffective teachers are ineffective because they've *stopped* struggling. Teaching is hard, and struggle is necessary in order to do it well. Your job is not to make teaching easy. Your job is not to remove the struggle. Your job is to make the struggle productive.

Carefully Plan Opportunities for Practice

One of the major differences between effective and ineffective teachers is that effective teachers have highly developed mental models for effective teaching and poor teachers do not. Ineffective teachers have a general understanding of how teaching works and are familiar with a few teaching moves but do not know how to integrate them into a fully articulated system or approach to teaching. Effective teachers understand not just the individual teaching moves but how these moves interact. They appreciate the subtle ways that the shifting factors of the classroom work together to influence or inhibit learning and know how to adjust teaching performance to enhance or mitigate these factors.

It isn't enough to show teachers a particular teaching move or strategy or to explain the principles of effective instruction. You must also show teachers how to develop a framework on which they can hang their growing knowledge about teaching. The framework helps them organize their growing knowledge in a way that makes it useful. It helps them see each new piece of information as a part of a larger picture and shows them where to store the new information. It helps them understand how to use what they are learning to make better predictions, anticipate confusion, solve problems on the spot, and ultimately, develop mastery.

Distinguish Between Training and Coaching

Use training for large skills and mentors and coaches for specific subskills. Training programs determine the general direction of development; coaching and mentoring provide teachers with detailed advice on which subskills need attention and how to apply what they have learned to their own practice.

Build Trust

It doesn't matter how skillfully you apply the strategies you have learned in this book; if people don't trust you, they will not follow your leadership. The strategies we've discussed engender trust, but it is important that you also work to establish and maintain trust with your staff. In order to build and maintain trust, you need to demonstrate consistency (people cannot trust what they cannot predict), transparency (people need to know that what they see is what they get), and coherence (people cannot trust what they don't understand).

Use Strategic Vulnerability

Most of us ask teachers to put themselves in vulnerable positions—asking them to be reflective during an evaluation conference, for example—without ever showing our own vulnerability. Great leadership is not built on invincibility; it is built on strategic vulnerability. Notice I said *strategic* vulnerability. People want to have confidence in their leaders, so this is not the time to trot out your every weakness and fault for the sake of showing that you are just like everyone else. What I mean is that you need to show teachers that you are learning too, that you are not perfect, that you don't have all the answers, and that you also learn from your mistakes. In other words, you need to acknowledge that you are human. Strategic vulnerability does not weaken your leadership; on the contrary, it helps teachers relate to you and trust you more.

Cultivate Discipline (Don't Dispense It)

Masterful teaching requires discipline—not the didactic accountability measures masquerading as discipline that we often impose on teachers but, rather, quiet, persistent, deliberate practice day in and day out. There's nothing heavy-handed about this discipline. It cannot be mandated; it must be cultivated.

Take Your Time

One of the major enemies of growth is impatience. You cannot grow your staff all at once and right away. Real growth, the kind that sticks, takes time and deliberate planning. It requires patience as you move all your teachers toward mastery. Just like a master teacher practices the principles until they become a natural response to students, a master leader practices principles until they become a natural response to teachers.

Focus on Quality, Not Quantity

Many reform models are based on the idea that if teachers just worked harder and longer, schools would be more successful. This linear thinking—more effort leads to greater results—is fundamentally flawed for two reasons. For one, we are not producing widgets here. We're helping students learn, and student learning is not nearly as quantifiable as we pretend. But, more important, this kind of leadership depletes energy and leaves teachers less equipped, less free to do what is best for children. The idea behind leading in a way that honors teachers' will and skill needs is really very simple: The more you meet teachers' will and skill needs, the more prepared and motivated they are to bring their very best to work each day and to give more of their best to their students. Focus your leadership efforts on getting not more work out of teachers but better work.

Stay the Course

Moving teacher will and skill is a marathon, not a sprint. I know that you have directives to execute, goals to reach, and AYP to make, and a significant amount of pressure to deal with. Although it may be tempting to reach for a quick solution that provides temporary relief from that pressure, quick solutions are not always sustainable, nor do they always have long-lasting impact. The work of building master teachers takes a considerable investment of time, energy, and commitment.

Leading Is Believing

Before you can help every teacher choose to become a master teacher, you must choose to believe that they can achieve mastery. You must choose to believe that everyone in your organization is valuable. Everyone—even the ones who don't pull their own weight or who currently do their jobs poorly. Everyone is valuable. They have a sphere of influence. They have the power to raise test scores or lower them. They have the power to irrevocably hurt or heal. They have the power to change your school for the better or—by their mediocrity, inaction, or terrible actions—lead your school to a slow but inevitable decline.

Schools are made up of people. The success or failure of your curriculum and organization and money and directives and reform models depends upon the people who must carry them out in individual classroom environments. If you want to transform your school, if you want to radically change its direction, you have to begin with changing the way that you see the people in it. You must believe, and you must help your teachers believe, that if they do the work with intense focus over time, they will become master teachers. This belief must permeate everything you do.

We say we want schools where every student can and does achieve, but do we really believe that such schools exist? It's hard for us to believe in such a school when our professional culture is built on the opposing idea: that great teachers are born, that the drive to be great is innate, and that there is little hope an ineffective teacher can improve. If we don't really believe in every teacher, it's a lot harder to believe in every kid.

The work of building a culture where every child is expected to succeed and does doesn't begin with the kids; it begins with us. Teachers who are worried about keeping their jobs can't be fully focused on helping students learn. Teachers who are convinced that they cannot get better are hard-pressed to believe that students can. Teachers who see their setbacks as evidence they lack the necessary gift will give up on themselves and their students. If teachers believe that their performance is for-ever constrained by their innate ability, their lack of talent, or their lack of some mysterious gift, they will never put in the work to improve. Why should they?

We tend to substitute working harder for getting better. Schools are cropping up whose entire ethos is that their teachers work really hard. Working really hard will get you short-term gains, but eventually, these young passionate teachers you recruited will burn out. What if, instead, you built a group of people who rather than simply working hard, worked hard at the right things so that teaching got easier—much easier—the harder they worked? What if you could create a culture built not on work-ing until you burn out but on working until you get better? What if you could create a professional learning environment where mastery was the norm, not some rare event that happened once or maybe twice in a career?

The answer is that you'd find your leadership practices are more in line with your values. You'd get reconnected to the reasons you wanted to be an educator to begin with. You'd learn that real leadership doesn't require a choice between doing your job and honoring the human beings you serve: You can do both. You'd discover ways to inspire the uninspired and cultivate passion for teaching in those who have largely given up. You'd rediscover your own passion and learn how to nurture and main-tain it so that you will never lose it again.

If you make this investment, yes, you will work harder. You will strug-gle to help some teachers choose mastery over mediocrity. You will get frustrated and want to give up and revert to old behaviors. You will meet a teacher who challenges your beliefs, and you will question yourself in the process. You will make mistakes, and you will get it wrong some-times. There will be days when you will wonder if this investment is really worth it.

The idea of leading in a way that honors will and skill is simple, but practice is required to do it well. You will face challenges, but if you prac-tice, it will get easier. Soon, you'll look up and realize that you don't have to try to lead this way; it has become your natural response to teachers.

Why make this investment? When you treat people with trust and respect, not only are they more engaged, they perform better. When you honor the people you lead, you perform better. Even more important, leading this way gives our students the teachers they deserve. Our students deserve to learn in classrooms where their teachers are getting better every day. They deserve teachers who believe that anyone can get better at anything with the right kind of support and who manifest this belief in their interactions with their students. They deserve teachers who are their best selves and consistently give the best of themselves to their students. They deserve, in short, *master teachers*.

So why make this investment? With the right kind of leadership, support, and practice, *any teacher* can become the kind of teacher our students deserve, and every student in every classroom will have the benefit of excellent instruction.

APPENDIX: TOOLS

Tool 1: A Diagnostic to Identify a Teacher's Skill Level

Tool 2: A Diagnostic to Identify a Teacher's Primary Will Driver

Tool 3: A Diagnostic to Identify Your Primary Will Driver

Tool 4: A Template for a Targeted Development Plan

Tool 5: Strategies for Tracking Skill Development

Tool 6: Strategies for Time Management

Tool 7: Strategies for Fostering Collaboration

TOOL 1

A Diagnostic to Identify a Teacher's Skill Level

Teacher Name: _____ Subject/Grade Level: _____

1. When planning lessons and discussing curriculum issues, this teacher tends to

   a. Focus on covering the curriculum exactly as it is written in the curriculum guide.
   b. Focus on covering as much as possible in the time allotted.
   c. Focus on helping students master all of the standards.
   d. Focus on helping students master all the standards and adapt their learning to a real-world context.

2. This teacher's pedagogical knowledge and approach can best be described as

   a. Limited. This teacher seems unaware of the range of approaches suitable to student learning.
   b. Fair. This teacher demonstrates some pedagogical knowledge but uses a limited range of approaches, some of which seem like a poor match for students' needs or the demands of the discipline.
   c. Effective. This teacher uses a wide range of pedagogical approaches that suit students' needs and the demands of the discipline.

    d. Extensive. This teacher uses a wide range of effective pedagogical approaches that are specific to each discipline and meet individual student needs.

3. This teacher's content knowledge can be best described as

    a. Limited. This teacher makes errors or fails to correct student errors.

    b. Proficient. This teacher seems aware of the important concepts of the curriculum but unsure of how these concepts relate to one another.

    c. Solid. This teacher seems to understand the key concepts of his/her discipline and how they relate.

    d. Extensive. This teacher seems to understand the key concepts of his/her discipline, how they relate to each other, and how they relate to other disciplines.

4. When supporting struggling learners, this teacher tends to

    a. Let students fail; there doesn't seem to be a plan for remediation.

    b. Use supports that are general and remedial in response to a pattern of poor performance.

    c. Provide most students with practice and individualized support through thoughtful design of classroom activities, although some students fall through the cracks and require intense remediation.

    d. Proactively and systematically catch students before they get into a free fall of failure and gradually remove supports as students become more proficient.

5. In using classroom assessments, this teacher tends to

    a. Focus almost exclusively on summative assessments that measure low-level knowledge and lack rigor.

    b. Take a perfunctory approach. Although assessment may be integrated into learning activities, goals for assessment are not entirely clear, the assessment format may not match instruction, and the assessment may not address all of the content.

   c. Align assessments and learning activities to learning goals most of
       the time, make assessment criteria clear and accessible to students,
       and gather formative assessment data.
   d. Plan assessments that are directly related to unit objectives, respond
       actively to student data, and adjust instruction accordingly.

6. When it comes to classroom management, this teacher

   a. Allows the students to run the classroom; rules are absent or
       unenforced.
   b. Seems inconsistent, showing favoritism to some students while
       ignoring or censuring others or enforcing some rules while letting
       others slide.
   c. Enforces rules with clear consequences and is able to quickly redi-
       rect student behavior and get students back on task.
   d. Implements discipline that is unobtrusive and preventative. Classes
       run smoothly and without disruption.

7. In general, this teacher's lessons tend to

   a. Focus on curriculum coverage and task completion.
   b. Be pitched too high or too low for students' current abilities or fea-
       ture expectations that seem low for some students and high for
       others.
   c. Address the learning standards with clear objectives, include rele-
       vant and appropriate questions that foster student thinking, provide
       clear explanations of the content, and make connections between
       the content, related content, and students' own prior knowledge
       and experiences.
   d. Move students in a steady progression toward rigorous unit
       learning goals and curricular standards and invite students to be
       co-creators of their learning experiences.

8. In terms of expectations, this teacher

   a. Conveys low expectations of students through the types of assign-
       ments he/she uses, negative interactions with students, and a fail-
       ure to hold students accountable for their behavior.
   b. Substitutes entertaining students for true cognitive engagement;
       students may not be able to tell the difference.

   c. Sets and holds students to rigorous standards and pushes students to reach beyond their current abilities but may step in to rescue students when they struggle or seem out of their depth.

   d. Helps students internalize rigorous learning standards, high expectations, and respect for themselves and others, and sets up learning experiences that allow students to take the lead in their own learning.

9. The overall flow of this teacher's classroom can best be described as

   a. Teacher-centered and teacher-directed; students aren't asked to contribute or engage.

   b. Uneven. Classes have a recognizable structure, but they do not always adhere to this structure uniformly throughout the lesson.

   c. Efficient, with very little loss of instructional time.

   d. Fluid and seamless.

10. When it comes to working with students, this teacher generally

   a. Takes a standard approach that does not factor in students' personal currencies and interests.

   b. Tries to persuade students to leave their personal currencies and interests at home and embrace classroom currencies instead.

   c. Recognizes and expresses appreciation for the currencies students bring with them to the classroom but focuses on helping them acquire new currencies rather than showing them how to use the currencies they have already.

   d. Focuses on helping each student leverage personal currencies to reach rigorous learning goals.

11. In discussions of expectations for students, this teacher tends to

   a. Express definitive opinions about what certain groups of students are and are not capable of doing.

   b. Speak about expectations in general and sometimes stereotypical terms, without mentioning specific students or specific plans for improving their achievement.

   c. Mention individual students' strengths, challenges, and learning needs and express the hope and intention to help these students meet high standards.

    d. Talk more about specific plans to help individual students than about students' current abilities.

12. This teacher's typical response to feedback from you is

    a. No response. This teacher does not seem to take note of feedback or use it in any way.

    b. Reactive. This teacher responds in emotional ways and has to be reminded that feedback is an opportunity to improve professional practice.

    c. Responsive. This teacher uses feedback to adjust professional practice.

    d. Proactive. This teacher uses feedback to adjust professional practices and actively seeks out additional feedback from you, students, parents, peers, and other supervisors.

13. When it comes to professional development, this teacher seems to

    a. Engage in it reluctantly or avoid it altogether; does not put the new ideas or approaches presented into practice.

    b. Engage in it randomly; sometimes incorporates the new ideas or approaches into practice and sometimes does not.

    c. Engage in it enthusiastically; consistently incorporates the new ideas or approaches into practice.

    d. Proactively seek it out and use action research to inform and improve practice.

14. When it comes to seeking resources to support students, this teacher tends to

    a. Not seek them at all. This teacher has expressed ignorance of available resources or uncertainty of how to use them to help students or to grow professionally.

    b. Rely heavily on school-based resources and accept and use them when they are made available.

    c. Examine all kinds of approaches and solutions and focus on finding the right one for students.

    d. Create individualized solutions for students by adapting existing resources to meet students' needs.

15. Based on your observations, this teacher tends to make instructional decisions based on

    a. What is most comfortable personally.
    b. What's most beneficial for students at this particular grade level.
    c. What's most beneficial for the various subgroups within the class (e.g., struggling students, on-target students, advanced students, English language learners).
    d. What's most beneficial for individual students.

16. In general, the students in this teacher's classroom are

    a. Distracted and disengaged.
    b. Minimally engaged. Students need constant supervision and repeated cues to stay on task.
    c. Engaged and productive most of the time.
    d. Actively involved in co-creating their learning experience—asking questions, making connections, setting goals, seeking feedback, and suggesting new ideas and directions for study.

17. This teacher's overall practice can best be described as

    a. Incoherent. You see little or no direction, consistency, or soundness to this teacher's instructional choices.
    b. Uneven. You've seen that this teacher has a limited repertoire of strategies and sometimes seems to apply these approaches randomly.
    c. Efficient. You've seen that instructional transitions are smooth, clear routines are in place and adhered to most of the time, and behavioral expectations are clear and generally met.
    d. Seamless and fluid. Good teaching seems effortless, as if it's this teacher's natural response to students.

Results: If you chose mostly
a's – It is likely that this teacher is a ***novice*** teacher.
b's – It is likely that this teacher is an ***apprentice*** teacher.
c's – It is likely that this teacher is a ***practitioner.***
d's – It is likely that this teacher is a ***master teacher.***

TOOL 2

A Diagnostic to Identify a
Teacher's Primary Will Driver

Teacher Name: _____ Subject/Grade Level: _____

1. On which of the following does this teacher tend to compliment you the most?

   a. How well you are managing the building.
   b. How clear your vision is or the values you express and exhibit.
   c. How you provide support and independence.
   d. How well you relate to staff, students, and parents.

2. If you were to give this teacher a new curriculum to implement, which of the following concerns would most likely be raised?

   a. How hard the new curriculum will be to implement.
   b. How pointless the new curriculum is.
   c. How the new curriculum will interfere with personal teaching style or process.
   d. How there is not enough time to sit down as a group and figure out the best way to approach the new curriculum and discuss what everyone plans to do.

3. If you were to recognize this teacher for a job well done, which would be valued most?

   a. Public praise and a certificate of accomplishment.

b. Mention of how the teacher's actions made a difference.

c. More independence.

d. Personal acknowledgment and appreciation from you, colleagues, or students.

4. Which of the following requests is most common from this teacher?

a. Additional training or opportunities to attend outside workshops.

b. A justification for a policy or mandate.

c. More free time or permission to modify a task.

d. More time to collaborate.

5. This teacher's primary goal seems to be

a. To master effective instruction or become a grade-level or subject-area expert.

b. To improve the lives of students.

c. To achieve more independence in the classroom, or to provide students with more control over their own lives.

d. To build effective relationships with others.

6. This teacher's strongest suit is

a. Effective use of strategies.

b. A real commitment to the work.

c. The ability to work independently and get things done.

d. Relationships with students, families, and colleagues.

7. This teacher's biggest weakness is

a. Ineffective use of instructional strategies.

b. A lack of commitment to the work.

c. The insistence on working independently and the tendency to "go rogue."

d. Difficult relationships with students, families, and colleagues.

8. When seeking feedback from you, this teacher's underlying question is really

   a. "Did I do it right?"
   b. "Was my contribution valuable?"
   c. "Did my way work?"
   d. "Do you like/respect me?"

9. The questions this teacher tends to raise in response to any new initiative are typically about which of the following?

   a. "What is the goal, and what are the criteria for success?"
   b. "Why are we doing this work?"
   c. "How will we be asked to meet the goal?"
   d. "Who will be involved, and how will it affect them?"

10. When working with students, this teacher's primary concern seems to be

   a. Helping students meet the standards.
   b. Helping students meet their full potential.
   c. Helping students become independent thinkers and learners.
   d. Helping students develop good relationships with teachers and each other.

Results: If you chose mostly
a's – This teacher's primary will driver is probably **mastery.**
b's – This teacher's primary will driver is probably **purpose.**
c's – This teacher's primary will driver is probably **autonomy.**
d's – This teacher's primary will driver is probably **belonging.**

TOOL 3

A Diagnostic to Identify
Your Primary Will Driver

1. Which of the following aspects of your leadership is most important to you?

    a. How well you are managing the building.
    b. The vision you have for your school and your students' learning.
    c. Being able to set your own priorities and pursue your own initiatives free from excessive oversight.
    d. How well you relate to staff, students, and parents.

2. Your district has just issued a new mandate. Which of the following scenarios would frustrate you the most?

    a. The new mandate will be difficult or nearly impossible to accomplish in the time or with the resources you currently have.
    b. The mandate seems absolutely pointless.
    c. The mandate will mean adjusting your leadership style and the goals that you have for your school.
    d. The mandate will upset your staff and do damage to the overall school climate.

3. If you were to be recognized for doing an excellent job with your school, which of the following rewards would you value most?

    a. Public praise, a certificate of accomplishment, or a monetary award.

    b. The personal satisfaction that you did something that mattered.

    c. Official license and funding to pursue a project for your school that you want to work on.

    d. Personal acknowledgment from your immediate supervisor.

4. Which of the following requests do you tend to make the most of your supervisor?

    a. Additional training or opportunities to attend outside workshops.

    b. A justification for a policy or mandate.

    c. More free time or permission to modify a task.

    d. More opportunities to collaborate with your colleagues.

5. Your professional goals tend to involve

    a. Mastering a particular skill set or reaching a new level of achievement.

    b. Reaching a particular ideal—typically one that aligns with your own passion for education and your own deeply held values.

    c. Becoming your own boss, or gaining the authority necessary to accomplish what you feel is most important.

    d. Building effective relationships and attaining the admiration and respect of your colleagues.

6. Your strongest suit is

    a. Effective use of leadership strategies and creative problem solving.

    b. A real commitment to the work and a passion for education.

    c. The ability to work independently and get things done.

    d. Effective relationships with students, families, and colleagues.

7. The teachers who tend to drive you the craziest are those who

    a. Refuse to improve or seem disinterested in getting better at their jobs.

    b. Seem to lack passion for teaching or commitment to their students.

    c. Seem needy and always want your attention.

    d. Seem cold, distant, and uninterested in making a connection with you or their students.

8. When seeking feedback from others, what you really want to know is

   a. "Did I do it right?"
   b. "Was my contribution valuable?"
   c. "Did my way work?"
   d. "Do you like/respect me?"

9. Which of the following questions do you usually raise in response to a new initiative?

   a. "What is the goal, and what are the criteria for success?"
   b. "Why are we doing this work?"
   c. "How will we be asked to meet the goal?"
   d. "Who will be involved, and how will it affect them?"

10. When working with teachers, it is most important to you that you

   a. Help them consistently hone their craft and grow toward mastery.
   b. Inspire them to better serve students and the mission, ideals, and goals of education.
   c. Help them meet their own individual potential by learning how to think and work more independently rather than relying on prescribed strategies and canned approaches.
   d. Establish positive relationships with them and ensure that they feel valued and supported.

11. Which of the following represents your worst nightmare?

   a. Not being good at your job, or failing in some key area.
   b. Doing work that doesn't make sense, seems pointless, and does not align with your personal beliefs or values.
   c. Being micromanaged.
   d. Being hated by those you lead or resented by your colleagues.

Results: If you chose mostly
a's – Your primary will driver is probably **mastery.**
b's – Your primary will driver is probably **purpose.**
c's – Your primary will driver is probably **autonomy.**
d's – Your primary will driver is probably **belonging.**

TOOL 4

A Template for a
Targeted Development Plan

This simple template can help you map out a plan for professional development that addresses a specific aspect of teacher skill and incorporates the eight approaches outlined in Chapter 3. For an example of the kind of improvement plan you want—one that isolates the root causes of a teacher's ineffectiveness and offers developmental, deliberate, and differentiated practice and support, see Figure 3.3 (p. 67).

This template is available for download at www.mindstepsinc.com/lead.

Goal: *(What do you hope to accomplish with this plan?)*		
Opportunities for Professional Development *(Include dates/frequency)*	**Characterized by** *(What steps will you take?)*	**Resulting in** *(How will you know if it is working?)*
Evaluation		
Elaboration		
Observation		
Practice		
Feedback		
Coaching		
Collaboration		
Reflection		

TOOL 5

Strategies for
Tracking Skill Development

1. One-to-One Targeted Tracking

The following is an example of an **individual tracking sheet** you might maintain to guide and document the professional development and skill growth of an individual teacher. This form is available as a free download at www.mindstepsinc.com/lead.

Notice that this spreadsheet is set up to focus on a single area for growth. This target might come from the teacher's personal professional growth plan, from past evaluations, or from a general acknowledgment of what this teacher needs to move to the next highest skill-level category. Additional targets might be tracked on different sheets within the same electronic file. For example, Mr. Flowers would have a single development file for the school year, with each of his target areas identified and his progress tracked for each.

Note, too, that the form is set up to prompt consideration of the eight essential professional development approaches discussed in Chapter 3 (see p. 45) and to document both the informal and formal feedback provided to the teacher (by you or by peers, as shown). It can help you plan follow-up professional development opportunities that will support the next step in the teacher's development and serve as documentation to support accountability.

Teacher: Mr. Flowers
Target Area for Growth: Rigor

DATE	FEEDBACK	PD OPPORTUNITIES	FOLLOW-UP ACTION	ADDITIONAL COMMENTS
10/13	Lessons still are not reaching the grade-level expectations. Need to make sure that you are teaching to the standard.	☐ *Evaluation* ☐ *Elaboration* ☒ *Observation* Peer observation with Ms. Glen on 10/16. ☐ *Practice* ☐ *Coaching* ☒ *Collaboration* Follow-up team planning on next unit. ☐ *Reflection*	Bring him in for a reflective conversation on Ms. Glen's feedback. Review and provide feedback on team plans.	Do a brief check-in to make sure that there will be enough time for a follow-up discussion. Offer release time if necessary.
10/30	Good job acknowledging the standard and making some connections. How can you help students make similar connections on their own throughout the lesson?	☒ *Evaluation:* Review evaluation instrument to emphasize the importance of student ownership. ☐ *Elaboration* ☐ *Observation* ☐ *Practice* ☐ *Coaching* ☐ *Collaboration* ☐ *Reflection*	Plan lesson that moves students to more ownership over the standards.	None

2. Whole-Staff Collaborative Tracking

If you are carrying out teacher development as part of a collaborative leadership team, it makes sense to coordinate your efforts. This way, teachers get consistent feedback, and school leaders are better able to track each teacher's growth. The following is an example of a **whole-staff collaborative tracking sheet** that leadership teams might use to capture and monitor feedback to all the teachers on staff. Go to www.mindstepsinc.com/lead for a free download of this form.

The idea is that individual members of the team will add to the file during the week, and then the whole team will meet at the end of the week to discuss trends and next steps for each teacher. Column 1 is set up to show each teacher's name. Column 2 lists the target skill for that teacher. Columns 3 and 5 are where members of the leadership team add observations about the teacher or feedback provided to the teacher that week. Notice that each team member includes his or her initials. Each new team member who visits the teacher's classroom can review the remarks of other team members before entering his or her own. Columns 4 and 6 provide space for team members to note any follow-up they or the teacher needs to do, as well as any due dates. This provides a more comprehensive record of the professional development efforts and helps to ensure follow-through and accountability for each teacher.

1	2	3	4	5	6
Teacher	Target Skill	Feedback (week of March 5)	Next Steps	Feedback (week of March 12)	Next Steps
Ms. Aspen	Classroom management	Establish routines for passing back papers. –PZ	Follow-up visit 3/7	Routines in place but not uniformly enforced. –KL	Work with instructional coach for strategies.
Mr. Beech	Pacing	On lesson plans, include time spans for each activity. –KL	Lesson plan review on Friday	Pacing still off. Too much time spent on preliminaries. Need to get warm-up down to 5 minutes. –DW	Work with instructional coach to develop a more efficient warm-up process.
Miss Cedar	Student ownership	Allow students to work in numbered pairs to correct homework. –DW	Share online resource for using numbered pairs.	Effective use of numbered pairs in correcting homework. –PZ	Follow-up reflective conversation about the effect of more student ownership on classroom climate.
Mr. Dogwood	Assimilate rigorous questioning with better feedback	Pre-plan questions for next lecture. –KL	Review lecture plans with teacher.	Level of questions in classroom is significantly improved. –KL	Provide additional resources on effective questioning techniques.
Ms. Elm	Lesson planning	Use the lesson planning template provided. –DW	Lesson plan review with coach.	Lesson plans use template, but parts are missing. –DW Lessons still disjointed and lack focus. –PZ	Submit lesson plans for the following week by Wednesday. Feedback meeting on Thursday.

TOOL 6

Strategies for Time Management

The biggest concern I hear about my approach to instructional leadership is not a philosophical objection to the process but a question about feasibility. More specifically, it's about time. With everything else a school leader has to do, how do you find the time to diagnose every teacher's skill and will, and then work with them to develop, motivate, and support them on their path toward mastery? Here are a few tips and strategies to help.

1. Use Your Team

Many instructional leaders get overwhelmed by the demands of their jobs because they try to go it alone. The schools where I have seen the most success in managing this process are those schools that share the work among the entire instructional leadership team. Some schools divide the professional development responsibilities among the administrators, instructional coaches, and teacher leaders such as team leaders or department heads. Others coordinate an observation schedule so that teachers are seen more frequently by a variety of the instructional leaders involved. Other administrators access district resources such as districtwide coaches or instructional leaders or even university partners and include them in their plans.

Bottom line: *You don't have to do this alone.* Get creative and invite other members of your school-based or district leadership team or involve outside partners as a part of your coordinated plan. Teaming up and dividing the workload can be the way to ensure all teachers get the attention they deserve.

2. Use the Master Schedule

Some leaders I have worked with use their master schedules to plan when they will observe and meet teachers. They create a table similar to the one below. In Column 1, they list the instructional periods or hours in the day. In Column 2, they list all the teachers who have planning periods during that time. These are the teachers who will be available at that time to stop in and see, schedule post-observation conferences with, provide feedback to, or otherwise work with. In Column 3, they list the teachers who are teaching during that period (and even what they are teaching) so that a leader can more efficiently plan observations, walk-throughs, and informal classroom visits.

Period	Teachers Planning	Teachers Teaching
Period One	Mr. Harris Ms. Jones Ms. Langston	Mr. Isaacs Ms. King Ms. Manning Mr. Neal Ms. Orlando
Period Two	Ms. Penny Mr. Reynolds Ms. Tinley	Mr. Quarles Miss Smyth Ms. Underwood Mr. Viarra Ms. Watts
Period Three	Etc.	

3. Use the Small Parts of the Day

Instead of looking for large swaths of time and waiting until you have an uninterrupted hour to give teachers feedback or provide follow-up support, look for and take advantage of small bits of time you might have throughout the day: during bus duty, when the two of you are standing and waiting for the buses to leave the parking lot; during class changes, when you are both standing in the hall watching students hurry to class;

during lunch duty, while you are both watching students throw away their trash; or even while you chaperone the JV volleyball game. Take these opportunities to check in with teachers, provide quick feedback from a walk-through, or offer advice. While this won't work in situations where your feedback is more confidential, it is a great way to stay connected with teachers and provide bits of guidance that will keep them moving forward.

4. Use Technology the Right Way

I worry sometimes about administrators and coaches who are so immersed in their technology and in taking notes during observations that they miss half of what is happening in the classroom. For shorter observations, it is better to sit and absorb what is happening and then write down your notes once you leave.

I find that technology is best used for scheduling conferences and follow-up visits, providing a written record of your verbal feedback, and keeping track of what you are working on with each teacher (see Tool 4). Technology is also a great way to create spaces for collaboration (see Tool 5), to provide teachers with observation opportunities when their schedules do not permit live observations (e.g., video self-observations or observations of other classrooms and model lessons), and to provide short professional development through webinars and online courses.

TOOL 7

Strategies for Fostering Collaboration

No matter how much instructional support you provide, teachers need time to collaborate with their colleagues. Not only does collaboration allow teachers to learn from one another, it also builds teachers' capacity to manage their own professional growth.

The main obstacle to effective collaboration among teachers is time. Here are five easy ways you can make time work for you to foster more collaboration in your building.

1. Use Dedicated Time

Be deliberate about collaboration. Offer time to collaborate during faculty meetings or other contractually obligated time. You might set aside the first 20 minutes of every staff meeting or the last hour of a professional development day for collaboration and co-planning. Once you set your policy, stick with it.

2. Use Online Chats

Teachers can collaborate electronically using synchronous or asynchronous chat features to discuss strategies or pursue topics of interest. This opens up the possibility of working "together" from home, but it also allows quick check-ins and conversation, classroom to classroom.

3. Use Video

Teachers can record themselves teaching a lesson and then send it to their colleagues for comments or suggestions. This is a way to reap the benefits of observation-based peer feedback without the difficulty of juggling schedules and securing substitutes.

4. Use a Work-in-Progress Protocol

Establish a process in which each week, one or two teachers on an established team (e.g., grade-alike teams or members of a professional learning community) bring in something they are working on—perhaps a new instructional strategy, a new lesson plan, or a new planning approach. They present what they are working on, why they chose that particular approach, and what they hope it will accomplish with their students. After each teacher's brief presentation (no more than 3 minutes), that teacher must listen quietly as the rest of the teachers in the group provide feedback or attempt to improve the strategy in some way. At the end of the discussion (which may last anywhere from 5 to 20 minutes), the original teacher presenter responds to colleagues' feedback, asks clarifying questions, and thanks the group for their input. Then the teacher goes back to the classroom, implements and finishes the work, and reports back to the group.

5. Use an "All-Day Staff Meeting"

In many schools, teachers who do not share the same planning period have difficulty finding time to work together. At Mindsteps, we've arrived at a creative solution to help schools get around the limitations of their master schedules—the "All-Day Staff Meeting." No, this *isn't* a single faculty meeting that lasts all day; it's a time-swapping arrangement. The information and topics you would typically cover with all teachers during an after-school meeting you instead discuss with small groups of teachers in a series of meetings held during their regular planning period. This frees the faculty meeting time after school for teacher collaboration and co-planning.

REFERENCES

Barth, R. (2005). *On common ground: The power of professional learning communities.* Bloomington, IN: Solution Tree.

Blase, J., & Blase, J. (1998). *Handbook of instructional leadership: How really good principals promote teaching and learning.* Thousand Oaks, CA: Corwin.

Colvin, G. (2006, October 30). What it takes to be great. Fortune, 154(9). Retrieved from http://money.cnn.com/magazines/fortune/fortune_archive/2006/10/30/8391794/index.htm

Colvin, G. (2008). *Talent is overrated: What really separates world-class performers from everybody else.* New York: Portfolio.

Coyle, D. (2009). *The talent code.* New York: Bantam.

Danielson, C. (2011). *The Framework for Teaching evaluation instrument (2011 edition).* Princeton, NJ: The Danielson Group.

Ericsson, K. A., Krampe, R. T., & Tesch-Römer, C. (1993). The role of deliberate practice in the acquisition of expert performance. *Psychological Review, 100*(3), 363–406. Available: http://dx.doi.org/10.1037/0033-295X.100.3.363

Gladwell, M. (2002). *The tipping point: How little things can make a big difference.* Boston: Back Bay Books.

Hanushek, E. A. (2004). Economic analysis of school quality. *European Economy: Quality and Efficiency in Education, Special Report No. 3* (pp. 29–48). Brussels, Belgium: Directorate-General for Economic and Financial Affairs, European Commission.

Heath, C., & Heath, D. (2010). *Switch: How to change things when change is hard.* New York: Broadway Books.

Jackson, R. (2008). *The instructional leader's guide to strategic conversations with teachers.* Washington, DC: Mindsteps Inc.

Jackson, R. (2009). *Never work harder than your students and other principles of great teaching.* Alexandria, VA: ASCD.

Levin, J., & Nolan, J. F. (2009). *Principles of classroom management: A professional decision-making model* (6th ed.). Boston: Pearson.

Pink, D. H. (2009). *Drive: The surprising truth about what motivates us.* New York: Riverhead Books.

Reeves, D. B. (2001). *Crusade in the classroom: How George W. Bush's education reforms will affect your children, our schools.* New York: Simon & Schuster.

Reiss, K. (2006). *Leadership coaching for educators: Bringing out the best in school administrators.* Thousand Oaks, CA: Corwin.

Yendol-Hoppey, D., & Dana, N. (2010). *Powerful professional development: Building expertise within the four walls of your school.* Thousand Oaks, CA: SAGE.

INDEX

The letter *f* following a page number denotes a figure

ABOUT THE AUTHOR

 **Robyn R. Jackson, PhD,** is a former high school teacher and middle school administrator. She is the founder and president of Mindsteps Inc., a professional development firm for teachers and administrators that provides workshops and materials designed to help any teacher reach every student. Dr. Jackson is the author of *Never Work Harder Than Your Students and Other Principles of Great Teaching, The Differentiation Workbook,* and *The Instructional Leader's Guide to Strategic Conversations with Teachers,* as well as the how-to guides in the Mastering the Principles of Great Teaching series. You can sign up for Dr. Jackson's monthly e-newsletter at www.mindstepsinc.com, follow her on Twitter at @robyn_mindsteps, or reach her via e-mail at robyn@mindstepsinc.com.